PRACTICE & ASSESS GRAMMAR

GRADES 6-8

© 2018 Erin Cobb
imlovinlit.com

Credits
Author: Erin Cobb
Proofreader: Josh Rosenberg

Carson-Dellosa Publishing LLC
PO Box 35665
Greensboro, NC 27425 USA
carsondellosa.com

Visit *carsondellosa.com* for correlations to Common Core, state, national, and Canadian provincial standards.

978-1-4838-4940-9
01-176181151

Table of Contents

Teacher's Guide/FAQ

This resource is jam-packed with content specifically designed to practice and assess the lessons in the Interactive Grammar Notebook. So that these activities are grade-level appropriate, I have two books:

    Grades 4–5
    Grades 6–8

For each lesson, there is a 20-item practice, followed by a 20-item assessment. The items on the assessment are similar in content and in format to the items on the practice so that your students are prepared for each assessment.

Many lessons are two pages, so I run them front and back and recommend that you do the same whenever possible.

Since there are two or more similar worksheets for each lesson (one or two practices and one assessment), I have included this information at the top of each page. It either reads Practice or Assessment, followed by the level when two leveled practice pages are offered. The lesson number and topic are always in the title.

Name _____   Date _____

Lesson 5-1: Prepositions Practice
Level B

A. Understanding Prepositions
Match each preposition with its role.

s Practice
Level B

Grammar Practice & Assess FAQ

Will these worksheets teach the lessons for me?
No. These worksheets are meant to be used after the lesson is taught in order to practice and then assess students' knowledge and understanding of the content or skill. The Interactive Grammar Notebook includes lessons for each skill. This book includes worksheets for each.

Will I need to find stories and other resources to use with these printables?
No! These are no-prep, which means all of the passages and content are included. Copy and go!

Are these meant to prepare students for Common Core Assessments such as PARCC or Smarter Balanced?
No. These are not meant to be used as test prep, but as everyday practices and assessments.

I teach students for multiple years. Can I use these worksheets?
Yes! There will be two sets (see above) so simply purchase the book(s) relevant for your grades.

Name _____   Date _____

0.5: Parts of Speech Practice

A. Recognizing Parts of Speech
Match each word with the part of speech it represents.

_____ 1. Wow!   a. noun
_____ 2. he   b. verb
_____ 3. below   c. pronoun
_____ 4. really   d. adjective
_____ 5. nice   e. adverb
_____ 6. dog   f. conjunction
_____ 7. and   g. interjection
_____ 8. run   h. preposition

B. Identifying Parts of Speech
Write the part of speech for each word in the sentence.

9. Johannah really likes apples and cherries.

Johannah _____

really   _____

likes   _____

apples   _____

and   _____

cherries _____

10. December is my favorite month.

December _____

is   _____

my   _____

favorite _____

month   _____

C. Using Parts of Speech
For each sentence or phrase, write the part of speech that should go in the blank. Do not fill it in with a word, just with the part of speech the missing word should be.

(11) If _____ had told me five months ago I would make the soccer team, (12) I would have told you that you were _____ . (13) Today, you'd _____ right! (14) I just made the soccer _____ ! (15) _____ ! (16) I trained _____ all summer. (17) I asked kids who were already _____ the team to help me. (18) When it came time to try out, I did _____ best. (19) The _____ posted the list, and my name was on it! (20) Not only did I make the team, _____ I made varsity. This is all just so amazing for me!

     ©2015 Erin Cobb • CD-105007

Name _____   Date _____

0.5: Parts of Speech Assessment

A. Recognizing Parts of Speech

Read each statement. Write if it is true (T) or false (F).

_____   1. The word *so* is a conjunction.
_____   2. The word *above* is a preposition.
_____   3. The word *really* is an adjective.
_____   4. The word *yes* is an interjection.
_____   5. The word *adore* is a verb.

B. Identifying Parts of Speech

Write the part of speech for each word in the sentence.

6. Stacy's beautiful doll needs clothes.

Stacy's   _____
beautiful   _____
doll   _____
needs   _____
clothes   _____

7. She is hungry, so she will eat.

She   _____
is   _____
hungry   _____
so   _____
she   _____
will eat _____

C. Using Parts of Speech

For each sentence or phrase, write the part of speech that should go in the blank. Do not fill it in with a word, just with the part of speech the missing word should be.

(8) Next year, I am going to be in high _____ ! (9) It feels like yesterday _____ was in kindergarten. (10) _____ , does time fly! (11) _____ I will be graduating from high school. (12) Then, I will be _____ to college. (13) After that, I will get a _____ job. (14) I'll get married and _____ kids. (15) Before I know it, _____ will be going to high school. (16) Then, they'll go to college _____ get real jobs. (17) They'll have kids, and I'll be an _____ grandma! (18) Time sure does go _____ ! (19) I _____ it would slow down. (20) I like being in _____ grade.

Name _____   Date _____

Lesson 1-1: Capitalization Practice

A. Understanding Capitalization Rules

Determine which capitalization rule(s) are demonstrated by each sentence.

a. Capitalize the first letter of a proper noun.
b. Capitalize all significant words in titles of books and other media.
c. Capitalize the first letter of a sentence, even in a quotation.
d. Capitalize names of relatives that indicate family relationship.
e. Capitalize a title that precedes a name, but do not capitalize a title that follows a name.
f. Capitalize countries, nationalities, and languages.

_____ 1. Did you see the documentary about Abraham Lincoln on the Historical Channel?
_____ 2. How often do you play baseball?
_____ 3. My Aunt Harriet is going to France on Wednesday.
_____ 4. Congressman Sam Sanders and Rudy Garland, the governor, are coming to the benefit.
_____ 5. Have you ever read *Three Blind Mice* by Carolyn Johnson?

B. Applying Correct Capitalization

Decide whether each sentence follows the correct capitalization rules and write yes (Y) or no (N).

_____ 6. I need to head to Pop's One-Stop Shoppe and the Book Store today.
_____ 7. On tuesday, I have to go to Dulles International Airport to catch my flight.
_____ 8. French and German are my favorite european languages.
_____ 9. Rover, our new puppy, is a French dog.
_____ 10. I went to visit Uncle Sal and Aunt Harriet in Tennessee.

Lesson 1-1: Capitalization Practice

C. Using Correct Capitalization

Identify the incorrectly capitalized word in each sentence and write it correctly. If there is no error, write **NE**.

(11) This summer, I am going on the school trip to france! (12) Our band teacher, mrs. lovelace, is sponsoring the trip. (13) She booked it through international tours for Americans, a special company that sends students on international trips. (14) We'll start our trip in paris, france and then head to some other regions. (15) I'm really looking forward to visiting longchamp palace in Marseille. (16) I was hoping we could also go to cannes, where I might actually get to rub elbows with the movie stars who vacation there! (17) Unfortunately, it is not part of our trip. (18) Still, i know we will have a great time. (19) I need to brush up on my french before I go, though! (20) I bought *french for tourists* to help me out, so I hope I learn a good amount before the trip.

11. _____   16. _____

12. _____   17. _____

13. _____   18. _____

14. _____   19. _____

15. _____   20. _____

Name _____   Date _____

Lesson 1-1: Capitalization Assessment

A. Understanding Capitalization Rules
Determine which capitalization rule(s) are demonstrated by each sentence.

a. Capitalize the first letter of a proper noun.
b. Capitalize all significant words in titles of books and other media.
c. Capitalize the first letter of a sentence, even in a quotation.
d. Capitalize names of relatives that indicate family relationship.
e. Capitalize a title that precedes a name, but do not capitalize a title that follows a name.
f. Capitalize countries, nationalities, and languages.

_____ 1. Jan and Sue are going to London, England for their vacation this year.
_____ 2. French pastries are Uncle John's favorite dessert.
_____ 3. *The Mystery of Stacey Crew* was featured on *The New York Times* bestseller list.
_____ 4. Grandma Jane isn't really my grandma; she's my friend Sarah's grandma.
_____ 5. Ronnie's Burger Spot has the best french fries in the world.

B. Applying Correct Capitalization
Decide whether each sentence follows the correct capitalization rules and write yes (Y) or no (N).

_____ 6. Do you like Swedish meatballs or Italian meatballs better?
_____ 7. For Halloween, my Sister Stella is going to be a cat.
_____ 8. I used *German for Beginners* to brush up on my German.
_____ 9. I don't know about you, but I could really go for some of Aunt Martha's Beef Stew right now.
_____ 10. Santa Clara Beach in California is beautiful.

Lesson 1-1: Capitalization Assessment

C. Using Correct Capitalization

Identify the incorrectly capitalized word in each part of the sentence and write it correctly. If there is no error, write **NE**.

(11) Fourteen Years ago, something wonderful happened. (12) I entered the world! (13) I was born on the 8th of may. (14) My uncle James and aunt Jessica were some of the first people to meet me. (15) They traveled all the way from Newark, New jersey to be at (16) Saint mary's hospital in Birmingham, Alabama. (17) They also brought me my first book — *Hello sun* (18) by harriet stormer. (19) At the time, my Uncle worked for the author. (20) Because of this connection, he got mrs. Stormer to sign the book for me!

11. _____

12. _____

13. _____

14. _____

15. _____

16. _____

17. _____

18. _____

19. _____

20. _____

Lesson 1-2: Using Commas Practice

A. Understanding Comma Rules
Determine which comma rule(s) are demonstrated in each sentence.

a. Use a comma to separate three or more items or elements in a series.

b. Use a comma between two adjectives only when the word *and* could be inserted in its place.

c. Use a comma before and after a word or phrase that renames the noun.

d. Use a comma when a sentence begins with an introductory word or phrase such as *well, yes, therefore, for example,* or *on the other hand.*

e. Use a comma between a city and state and after the state if the sentence continues.

f. Use a comma to separate the day of the month from the year and after the year if the sentence continues.

g. Use a comma when a sentence begins with a prepositional phrase, adverbial clause, or dependent clause.

h. Use a comma to interrupt direct quotations or before or after a direct quotation.

_____ 1. On May 8, 2022, there will be a big parade in New York, New York.

_____ 2. "No, I don't want to go with you," Johnnie told his mother.

_____ 3. "Unless it snows, I'll go out at midnight to see the latest Drew Danger movie!"

_____ 4. "At the store, don't forget the flour, eggs, and butter," Mom reminded us.

_____ 5. "We need to buy ornaments, tinsel, and other decorations for the tree," my sister said. "For example, we could use a star for the top of the tree."

B. Applying Comma Rules
Determine whether each sentence uses a comma correctly and write yes (Y) or no (N).

_____ 6. I don't know what you want to make, but I'm sure I have chocolate bars, marshmallows, and graham crackers.

_____ 7. "Please block off April 3, 2019 on your calendar," said Mom. "We're going on a cruise!"

_____ 8. "Hey you guys," said the cop. "you need to wait for the light to change before crossing the street."

_____ 9. Every Thursday, my mom drives to Jackson, Mississippi, to visit her sister.

_____ 10. "Oh, please," my sister sighed, "like I'd actually wear your clothes."

Lesson 1-2: Using Commas Practice

C. Using Commas Correctly

For each sentence, decide where to add a comma. If no comma is needed, write **NC** for "no comma" above the sentence.

(11) "Whenever I make plans you always mess them up" my mom said to my dad. (12) "I mean it's not like you didn't know you had to work on Tuesday when I made the appointment," she continued. (13) My dad just sighed nodded his head and went back to working on his crossword puzzle. (14) "Well aren't you going to say anything?" my mom asked. (15) "What do you want me to say?" my dad replied. "I'm sorry?"

(16) My parents have been having the same fight every year since July 12 2005. (17) That's the first time my mom made an appointment on a Tuesday. Well that's the only day of the week my dad can't take off from work. (18) Since then she has made the same appointment on a Tuesday year after year. (19) My dad knows this but he never says anything. (20) Even if he said something my mom would never admit she was wrong. I suppose we'll just hear the same conversation on an annual basis!

Name _____   Date _____

Lesson 1-2: Using Commas Assessment

A. Understanding Comma Rules

Determine which comma rule(s) are demonstrated in each sentence.

a. Use a comma to separate three or more items or elements in a series.

b. Use a comma between two adjectives only when *and* could be inserted in its place.

c. Use a comma before and after a word or phrase that renames the noun.

d. Use a comma when a sentence begins with an introductory word or phrase such as *well, yes, therefore, for example,* or *on the other hand*.

e. Use a comma between a city and state/country and after the state/country if the sentence continues.

f. Use a comma to separate the day of the month from the year and after the year if the sentence continues.

g. Use a comma when a sentence begins with a prepositional phrase, adverbial clause, or dependent clause.

h. Use a comma to interrupt direct quotations and before (or after) a direct quotation.

_____ 1. Yes, I would like a milkshake, three double cheeseburgers, and a large salad.

_____ 2. Whenever it rains, my brother puts on his boots and goes outside to jump in the puddles.

_____ 3. Even though she likes apples, my sister won't eat applesauce, apple pie, or apple crisp.

_____ 4. I have lived in Paris, France since August 13, 2013.

_____ 5. My best friend only eats foods that are red, green, or blue, so her mom goes through a lot of food coloring.

B. Applying Comma Rules

Determine whether each sentence uses a comma correctly and write yes (Y) or no (N).

_____ 6. For example, I love hiking, biking, and running.

_____ 7. On Thursday, September 23 2018 you are invited to a dance.

_____ 8. Yes, I know it's important to remember to feed the fish, clean their tank, and add chemicals to the water.

_____ 9. "We should head to the movies after school," Alisha said.

_____ 10. "Don't be late" my dad called as he walked out the door.

 Grammar Practice & Assess • imlovinlit.com   ©2015 Erin Cobb • CD-105007

Lesson 1-2: Using Commas Assessment

C. Using Commas Correctly

For each sentence, decide where to add a comma. If no comma is needed, write **NC** for "no comma" above the sentence.

(11) Every summer my mom says "Pack your bags! We're heading on an adventure." (12) I never know where we're going to go but I always know it will be fun. (13) One summer we ended up in Fargo North Dakota. (14) We've also been to Oklahoma California, New York and many other states. (15) Since I never know where we're going I always pack a variety of clothes. (16) We never know if we'll end up somewhere with extremely cool summers. (17) Maybe we'll drive up to Alaska to the Northwest Territories or somewhere even farther north! (18) "The fun is in the adventure" my mom always says. (19) She's right. (20) I never know where we're going but I'm always ready to go there!

Name _____   Date _____

Lesson 1-3: Using Apostrophes Practice

A. Understanding the Rules

Write **P** next to each sentence if the word with an apostrophe is used to show possession.
Write **C** next to each sentence if the word with an apostrophe is used as part of a contraction.

_____ 1. My brothers' favorite activity is wrestling.

_____ 2. Where'd you put the salt and pepper shakers?

_____ 3. Don't you want to know what I got you for your birthday?

_____ 4. The bus's passengers were getting tired of sitting in traffic.

_____ 5. Why'd you purposely forget to get your brother a present?

B. Identifying Errors

Write **C** if the sentence uses apostrophes correctly and **IC** if it uses apostrophes incorrectly.

_____ 6. The students's textbooks did not arrive in time for school to start.

_____ 7. My grandparents' house was built in the 1850s.

_____ 8. Havent you always wanted to go to Paris?

_____ 9. Paris's lights are the most beautiful during the summertime.

_____ 10. The dog dug a hole and got mud stuck all over it's paws.

C. Using Apostrophes

For each sentence or phrase below, rewrite the word that needs an apostrophe correctly. If no apostrophe is needed, write **NA**.

11. _____   (11) Every November, Americans celebrate Thanksgiving.

12. _____   (12) Canadians have a Thanksgiving too, but it isnt in November.

13. _____   (13) Its in October and (14) was the first Thanksgiving celebration in

14. _____   the Americas. (15) The Canadians Thanksgiving took place 43 years

15. _____   before Thanksgiving in the United States. (16) Their first Thanksgiving

16. _____   was in the 1570s, (17) but Thanksgiving in the United States was

17. _____   in the 1620s. (18) There arent many differences between the two

18. _____   Thanksgivings. (19) People give thanks during both holidays. I doubt

19. _____   turkeys are giving thanks, though! (20) After all, both countries serve

20. _____   turkey on their Thanksgiving menus, which means many turkeys lives

are at stake in both countries. Whether it's October or November,

turkeys are just out of luck in North America!

Name _____   Date _____

Lesson 1-3: Using Apostrophes Assessment

A. Understanding the Rules

Write **P** next to each sentence if the word with an apostrophe is used to show possession.
Write **C** next to each sentence if the word with an apostrophe is used as part of a contraction.

_____ 1. Didn't you want to go to the movies tonight?

_____ 2. Damaris's cat doesn't like catnip.

_____ 3. How'd you do on Mr. Claus's test?

_____ 4. When's the last time you loaded the dishwasher?

_____ 5. Abraham Lincoln's top hat is iconic.

B. Identifying Errors

Write **C** if the sentence uses apostrophes correctly and **IC** if it uses apostrophes incorrectly.

_____ 6. Odysseus's struggle to get back home shaped his character.

_____ 7. Charles' speech failed to impress the student body.

_____ 8. We haven't eaten out in ages, so let's go out to eat tonight.

_____ 9. Il'l call my mom and ask if I can sleep over at your house tonight.

_____ 10. Wher'ed you put your brothers' shirt?

C. Using Apostrophes

For each sentence or phrase below, rewrite the word that needs an apostrophe correctly. If no apostrophe is needed, write **NA**.

11. _____

12. _____

13. _____

14. _____

15. _____

16. _____

17. _____

18. _____

19. _____

20. _____

(11) Laertes is a character in William Shakespeares Hamlet. (12) Laertess name comes from Greek mythology. (13) To the Greeks, he was best-known as Odysseuss father. (14) He was also the grandfather of Telemachus, who was his sons son. (15) However, in Hamlet, Laertes was Poloniuss son. (16) During Hamlet, Laertes doesnt react very well to Polonius's murder. (17) He gets a bunch of soldiers to storm the castle, which was a normal way of reacting in the 1500s. (18) He ends up fighting his sisters ex-boyfriend, Hamlet. (19) In the end, neither Hamlet nor Laertes gets the last LOL. (20) Of course, both men end up dead. Then again, anyone familiar with Shakespearean tragedies could predict that thats how Hamlet would end!

Name _____   Date _____

Lesson 1-4: Using Quotation Marks Practice

A. Understanding Quotation Marks
Determine which quotation mark rule(s) are demonstrated in each sentence.

a. Quotation marks should only be used for direct quotes, not indirect quotes.

b. Use a comma after a direct quotation in a sentence. Commas always go inside quotation marks.

c. Use a comma to introduce or interrupt direct quotations or after a direct quotation.

d. When a question is asked inside quotation marks, use a question mark instead of a comma. In a statement, always use a comma in place of the period.

e. Use quotation marks for titles of publications that are part of bigger publications.

f. When a question ends with a title in quotations, place the question mark outside of the quotation marks. Question marks and exclamation points only go inside of quotation marks if they are part of the quoted matter.

_____ 1. "You don't want to forget to do your homework," said Mrs. Johnson as she dismissed the class.

_____ 2. "How old are you?" asked the young boy.

_____ 3. Our class read an article called "The Five Senses" in *Science Kids* magazine.

_____ 4. Are you going to listen to "White Christmas"?

B. Recognizing Proper Use
Determine whether each sentence correctly uses quotation marks and write yes (Y) or no (N).

_____ 5. We sang "Happy Birthday" to my sister before she blew out her candles.

_____ 6. When I asked my dad what we were having for dinner, he said, "Wait and see!"

_____ 7. "How many cats do you have," my sister asked.

_____ 8. "All Day Long" is my favorite song on the band's new album.

_____ 9. "Well," he said, "I'll just go by myself."

Lesson 1-4: Using Quotation Marks Practice

C. Using Quotation Marks Correctly

Each sentence in the paragraph is missing quotation marks. Fill in the quotation marks in the correct places. If no quotation marks are needed, don't do anything to that sentence.

(10) Yesterday, the magazine I was reading featured an article about dogs called Dogs and Their Bones that talked about why dogs bury their bones. (11) The author interviewed a dog expert named Sara Keeler who said dogs bury their bones to keep them away from other dogs. (12) Dogs are very possessive, Keeler said. (13) After reading the article, I went to talk to my dog. (14) I asked him, Why do you bury your bones? (15) He looked at me and said, Arf! (16) What does that mean? I asked. (17) He looked at me and said, It means that I bury my bones because they taste better that way! (18) I was shocked to hear my dog actually talk. (19) I wrote a letter to Sara Keeler saying, Ms. Keeler, my dog says he buries his bones because they taste better that way, not to keep them away from other dogs. (20) She wrote back saying she would like to meet my talking dog one day!

Lesson 1-4: Using Quotation Marks Assessment

A. Understanding Quotation Marks
Determine which quotation mark rule(s) are demonstrated in each sentence.

a. Quotation marks should only be used for direct quotes, not indirect quotes.

b. Use a comma after a direct quotation in a sentence. Commas always go inside quotation marks.

c. Use a comma to introduce or interrupt direct quotations or after a direct quotation.

d. When a question is asked inside quotation marks, use a question mark instead of a comma. In a statement, always use a comma in place of the period.

e. Use quotation marks for titles of publications that are part of bigger publications.

f. When a question ends with a title in quotations, place the question mark outside of the quotation marks. Question marks and exclamation points only go inside of quotation marks if they are part of the quoted matter.

_____ 1. My teacher told me we wouldn't have any homework over the weekend.

_____ 2. Have you ever read the poem "A Snowy Night"?

_____ 3. "Where are you going?" my mom asked.

_____ 4. When I asked where she was going, my sister said, "I'm going to the store," before walking out the door.

_____ 5. "I'm not sure," Eric said, "what I'm going to do about your problem."

B. Recognizing Proper Use
Determine whether each sentence correctly uses quotation marks and write yes (Y) or no (N).
(**BONUS**: What rule does each sentence use or break? Write the letter from the rules in section A after each sentence.)

_____ 6. Who said, "The only thing we have to fear is fear itself"? (Bonus: _____)

_____ 7. My mom said, "Don't you want to go outside and play"? (_____)

_____ 8. We read a book of poems called "The Night Poems." (_____)

_____ 9. We read a poem called "Starry Night" in a book called *The Night Poems*. (_____)

_____ 10. "I like to drink pop," said Robert, "but I'm not allowed to drink it often." (_____)

Lesson 1-4: Using Quotation Marks Assessment

C. Using Quotation Marks Correctly

Many of the sentences in the paragraph are missing quotation marks. Fill in the quotation marks in the correct places. If no quotation marks are needed in a sentence, do nothing.

(11) Tomorrow, we are going to have a big test, said Mrs. Carter, (12) so you'd better study hard tonight. (13) Why do we have to take another test? asked Alisha. (14) Yeah, Lisa piped up, why can't we write a paper or something? (15) Mrs. Carter said she thought a paper was a good idea. (16) Tonight, said Mrs. Carter, instead of studying for your test, I want you to write a poem about your favorite song. (17) Joseph said he was going to write about Row, Row, Row Your Boat, (18) and Ben said he was going to write about The Farmer in the Dell. (19) What are you going to write about, Lisa? asked Mrs. Carter. (20) Lisa said she'd have to think about it.

Name _____   Date _____

Lesson 1-5: Using Numbers Practice

A. Recognizing Number Rules

Determine which number rule is demonstrated by each sentence.

a. Spell out numbers for numbers less than 10. Use numerals for numbers 10 and above. The same rule also applies to ordinal numbers.

b. Do not begin a sentence with a numeral. To avoid writing out long numbers, reword the sentence.

c. Spell out centuries and decades. Use numerals for years.

d. Do not abbreviate units of measurement. Write out the word *percent*.

e. When two numbers are next to each other, write out one of them.

f. Be consistent within the same sentence with the same types of numbers, even if you must break the first rule.

_____ 1. My cat just gave birth to five kittens.

_____ 2. The chef made three steaks, five salads, and eight potatoes.

_____ 3. She is in her nineties.

_____ 4. The recipe calls for three 16-ounce boxes of pasta.

_____ 5. All of their socks are 55 cents.

B. Identifying Correct Number Use

Determine whether the numbers are used correctly in each sentence and write yes (Y) or no (N).

_____ 6. We ordered 25 hamburgers.

_____ 7. I have seventy friends.

_____ 8. We need 35 twelve-inch rulers.

_____ 9. I bought 2 pairs of socks, 3 pairs of shoes, and 15 hair bows.

_____ 10. 2 kittens is too many.

Name _____   Date _____

Lesson 1-5: Using Numbers Practice

C. Writing Out Numbers Correctly

For each number given, write the correct form of the number.

(11) We already had _____ kittens in our family (12) when my cat had a litter of
                         (3)

_____ kittens. (13) That brought the grand total to _____ kittens. (14)
      (5)   (8)

_____ kittens get awfully hungry, (15) so we had to buy _____
      (8)   (25)

pounds of dry food (16) and _____ cans of wet food each week. (17) They also
                                   (50)

drink _____ gallons of water. (18) We have _____ litter boxes
            (35)   (2)

that hold (19) _____ pounds of kitty litter, (20) and it seems like the cats produce
                     (10)

_____ pounds of waste each week!
      (1,000)

Name _____   Date _____

Lesson 1-5: Using Numbers Assessment

A. Recognizing Number Rules
Determine which number rule is demonstrated by each sentence.

a. Spell out numbers for numbers less than 10. Use numerals for numbers 10 and above. The same rule also applies to ordinal numbers.

b. Do not begin a sentence with a numeral. To avoid writing out long numbers, reword the sentence.

c. Spell out centuries and decades. Use numerals for years.

d. Do not abbreviate units of measurement. Write out the word *percent*.

e. When two numbers are next to each other, write out one of them.

f. Be consistent within the same sentence with the same types of numbers, even if you must break the first rule.

_____ 1. The three-foot ladder was not tall enough to reach the roof.

_____ 2. The town celebrated its bicentennial in 2012.

_____ 3. We need 135 cookies for the bake sale.

_____ 4. We sold 35 cupcakes, 52 brownies, and 102 cookies.

_____ 5. I have two 5-year-old brothers.

B. Identifying Correct Number Use
Determine whether the numbers are used correctly in each sentence and write yes (Y) or no (N).

_____ 6. Is your birthday on December 10th?

_____ 7. The store is 5 miles down the road.

_____ 8. I took thirty-five hours to finish 3 quilts.

_____ 9. The forties are my favorite decade.

_____ 10. I'm excited about babysitting two toddlers!

Name _____   Date _____

Lesson 1-5: Using Numbers Assessment

C. Writing Out Numbers Correctly

For each number given, write the correct form of the number.

(11) _____ people make up our family. (12) My brother is _____,
          (6)   (2)

(13) my sister is _____, (14) I am _____, (15) my older brother is
                         (4)   (13)

_____, (16) my mom is _____, (17) and my dad is
       (18)   (38)

_____. (18) We have been a family of _____ since (19)
       (40)   (6)

_____, but next year, (20) we will be a family of _____!
     (2013)   (7)

Name _____   Date _____

Lesson 1-6: Using Plurals Practice

A. Recognizing Plural Rules

Match the noun ending with the way to form its plural. Note: Some endings will have more than one match.

_____ 1. *s*, *ss*, *ch*, *sh*, *x*, *z*; gas
_____ 2. *us*; nucleus
_____ 3. consonant + *o*; superhero
_____ 4. *f* or *fe*; life
_____ 5. consonant + *y*; pony
_____ 6. vowel + *y*; bay

a. add -*es*
b. change *y* to *i,* add -*es*
c. add -*s*
d. change *f* to *v,* add -*es*
e. change *us* to *i*

B. Identifying Plurals

Circle the incorrect plural.

7. a. ladies
   b. men
   c. tables
   d. fixs

8. a. zeroes
   b. symphonys
   c. monkeys
   d. stories

9. a. tornadoes
   b. crocodiles
   c. ferries
   d. soloes

10. a. geese
    b. moose
    c. mouses
    d. women

C. Forming Plurals

Form the plural of each word in parentheses.

The little (11) _____ (kid) were so excited! They were going to meet real-life (12) _____ (superhero)! The (13) _____ (child) were all big superhero (14) _____ (fan). They wrote (15) _____ (letter) explaining why they wanted to meet their (16) _____, (hero) and their (17) _____ (wish) were granted by some (18) _____ (man) in superhero (19) _____ (costume). They had the time of their (20) _____ (life).

Name _____   Date _____

Lesson 1-6: Using Plurals Assessment

A. Recognizing Plural Rules

Match the plural with the rule describing how to form its plural.

_____ 1. hatch   a. add -es
_____ 2. fairy   b. change y to i, add -es
_____ 3. mango   c. add -s
_____ 4. wife   d. change f to v, add -es
_____ 5. bully   e. change us to i
_____ 6. sea

B. Identifying Plurals

Circle the incorrect plural.

7. a. states   8. a. radios   9. a. dresses   10. a. boxes
    b. elves   b. bongos   b. mess'   b. taxs
    c. scarves   c. halos   c. stresses   c. axes
    d. scarfs   d. radioes   d. brooches   d. oxen

C. Forming Plurals

Form the plural of each word in parentheses.

(11) As the moon revolves around Earth, it looks like it changes shape in the sky. These changes in shape are called _____ (phase). (12) In different _____ (country), the phases of the moon look different. (13) For example, in the United States we see a crescent-shaped moon, but in _____ (place) near the equator, the moon looks like a smile. (14) In the past, different _____ (society) used lunar calendars to help tell time. (15) A lunar month is 29.53 _____ (day), but a regular month is around 30.44 days. Something unique, called an "eclipse," happens with the moon. (16) Solar and lunar _____ (eclipse) happen when the moon and sun pass in certain ways. (17) You can also see different _____ (feature) on the surface on the moon, depending on its phases. (18) The surface of the moon has _____ (crater) and other pits. (19) We call the moon's phases _____ (quarter), and they have been changing for _____ (century).

Name _____   Date _____

Lesson 1-7: Using Commonly Confused Words Practice

A. Recognizing Commonly Confused Words
Match each word with the word it is commonly confused with.

_____ 1. too
_____ 2. capitol
_____ 3. then
_____ 4. affect
_____ 5. principle

a. than
b. effect
c. to
d. capital
e. principal

B. Identifying Commonly Confused Words
Determine whether each commonly confused word is used correctly and write yes (Y) or no (N).

_____ 6. It's hard to adopt to a new environment.
_____ 7. I advise you to follow my advice.
_____ 8. We walked down the isle on the aisle.
_____ 9. He said "No girls allowed," aloud.
_____ 10. There not going the right way to get there.

C. Using Commonly Confused Words
Choose the correct word to complete each blank.

(11) After I fainted, the doctor checked to see if I was _____ (conscious/ conscience). (12) I had walked _____ (further/farther) than I should've (13) and ran out of _____ (breath/breathe). (14) I kept walking _____ (since/ sense) I thought the destination was closer. (15) Turns out, it was _____ (to/too/two) far for me. (16) I thought there was only one mile left, but really there were _____ (to/too/two). (17) Next time, I will stop and rest rather _____ (than/then) continuing on beyond my limits. (18) The _____ (effect/affect) of (19) walking _____ (to/too/two) far is not something I want to experience again. (20) At least I'm _____ (conscious/conscience) now!

Name _____   Date _____

Lesson 1-7: Using Commonly Confused Words Assessment

A. Recognizing Commonly Confused Words

Match each word with the word it is commonly confused with.

_____ 1. cite   a. sight
_____ 2. loose   b. breath
_____ 3. sense   c. lose
_____ 4. breathe   d. since
_____ 5. passed   e. past

B. Identifying Commonly Confused Words

Determine whether each commonly confused word is used correctly and write yes (Y) or no (N) .

_____   6. He was ready for his assent up the mountain.
_____   7. Everyone except Johnny was going on the field trip.
_____   8. It's time for the biggest adventure of your life.
_____   9. I'm sorry I can't except your gift.
_____   10. I don't want to lose the game.

C. Using Commonly Confused Words

Choose the correct word to complete each blank.

(11) Tomorrow, we are going to the _____ (altar/alter) to get married! (12) Everyone we know is going to be _____ (there/they're/their). (13) We will say our vows _____ (allowed/aloud) (14) after walking down the _____ (aisle/isle). (15) After the ceremony and reception, we will jet off to a tropical _____ (aisle/isle) (16) where _____ (there/they're/their) will be lots of sun. (17) I can't wait until that golden sand is in _____ (sight/cite/site)! (18) I'll _____ (breathe/breath) a sigh of relief (19) as I _____ (loose/lose) myself in the beauty of the (20) tropical _____ (aisle/isle).

Name _____   Date _____

Lesson 2-1: Four Types of Sentences Practice

A. Defining Types of Sentences
Match each sentence type with its description.

_____ 1. emotion or excitement   a. declarative
_____ 2. question   b. imperative
_____ 3. command or request   c. interrogative
_____ 4. statement   d. exclamatory

B. Identifying Types of Sentences
Identify each type of sentence.

_____ 5. Hey! I haven't seen you in a long time!   a. declarative
_____ 6. Stop singing.   b. imperative
_____ 7. I am a boy.   c. interrogative
_____ 8. Where have you been?   d. exclamatory
_____ 9. Don't forget to do your chores.
_____ 10. Is that a new shirt?

C. Punctuating Types of Sentences
Correctly punctuate each sentence. Then, write the sentence type.

(11) Did you know that the ability to invent tools is one of the unique characteristics of man _____ (12) Man has been inventing tools since ancient times _____ (13) It's pretty amazing _____ (14) Tools allowed early man to hunt, build things, and survive _____ (15) What kind of material do you think the earliest tools were made of _____ (16) They were made of stone _____ (17) Wow _____ (18) They could shape stone into all sorts of shapes ___ (19) Can you make tools out of stone _____ (20) Get out there and invent something today _____

11. _____   16. _____
12. _____   17. _____
13. _____   18. _____
14. _____   19. _____
15. _____   20. _____

Name _____   Date _____

Lesson 2-1: Four Types of Sentences Assessment

A. Defining Types of Sentences

Match each sentence type with its description.

_____ 1. imperative   a. statement

_____ 2. declarative   b. command

_____ 3. interrogative   c. emotion

_____ 4. exclamatory   d. question

B. Identifying Types of Sentences

Identify each type of sentence.

_____ 5. It's snowing outside.   a. declarative

_____ 6. Yes! I'd love to come!   b. imperative

_____ 7. Please don't sit in the broken chair.   c. interrogative

_____ 8. Why did you do that?   d. exclamatory

_____ 9. Come quickly.

_____ 10. Where'd you disappear to yesterday?

C. Punctuating Types of Sentences

Correctly punctuate each sentence. Then, write the sentence type.

(11) Have you ever had a dream ____ (12) What was that dream ____ (13) My dream is to go into outer space ____ (14) Outer space is so cool ____ (15) It's awesome ____ (16) I hope I can go into outer space someday ____ (17) What can I do to help make my dream come true ____ (18) Give me some ideas ____ (19) Those are awesome ____ (20) Now, go make your dream come true too ____

11. _____   16. _____

12. _____   17. _____

13. _____   18. _____

14. _____   19. _____

15. _____   20. _____

Name _____   Date _____

Lesson 2-2: Subject & Predicate Practice
Level A

A. Recognizing Subjects and Predicates
Determine whether each statement describes the complete subject, simple subject, complete predicate, or simple predicate.

_____ 1. One word that tells what the sentence is about

_____ 2. Multiple words that tell what the sentence is about

_____ 3. One action or linking verb that tells what something is or does

_____ 4. Multiple verbs and words that tell what something is or does

a. complete subject
b. simple subject
c. complete predicate
d. simple predicate

B. Identifying Subjects and Predicates
Determine what the underlined portion of the sentence represents.

5. The <u>big, mean dog</u> snarled at me.
   a. simple subject
   b. complete subject

6. Our wild and crazy <u>cat</u> chased his mouse.
   a. simple subject
   b. complete subject

7. <u>Long-haired hamsters</u> make great pets.
   a. simple subject
   b. complete subject

8. I <u>never needed</u> a passport until today.
   a. simple predicate
   b. complete predicate

9. My best friend <u>moved to China</u>.
   a. simple predicate
   b. complete predicate

10. <u>My best friends, Sally, Kara, and Marissa,</u> are all coming over for a sleepover.
   a. simple subject
   b. complete subject
   c. simple predicate
   d. complete predicate

 Grammar Practice & Assess • imlovinlit.com   ©2015 Erin Cobb • CD-105007

Lesson 2-2: Subject & Predicate Practice
Level A

C. Finding the Subject and Predicate

For each sentence, underline the subject or predicate listed in parentheses.

(11, simple subject) The Persians attacked Athens in 490 BC. (12, complete subject) The Persians were great fighters. (13, simple predicate) Everybody in Athens was frightened.

(14, complete predicate) The people of Athens had a democracy. (15, simple subject) They wanted an oligarchy. (16, simple predicate) Instead, they decided to fight the Persians.

(17, complete subject) They thought they would lose. (18, complete predicate) Actually, the Athenians beat the Persians. (19, simple subject) They tried a new way of fighting.

(20, simple predicate) Their new way of fighting worked.

Name _____   Date _____

Lesson 2-2: Subject & Predicate Practice

A. Recognizing Subjects and Predicates

Determine whether each statement describes the complete subject, simple subject, complete predicate, or simple predicate.

_____ 1. All of the words telling what the sentence is about

_____ 2. An action verb or linking verb describing what something is or does

_____ 3. A noun or pronoun telling what the sentence is about

_____ 4. All of the words telling what something is or does

a. complete subject
b. simple subject
c. complete predicate
d. simple predicate

B. Identifying Subjects and Predicates

Determine what the underlined portion of the sentence represents.

5. The angry holiday <u>elf</u> refused to make any toys.
   a. simple subject
   b. complete subject

6. <u>The happy-go-lucky child</u> wasn't upset by anything.
   a. simple subject
   b. complete subject

7. My ornery <u>brother</u> needs a job.
   a. simple subject
   b. complete subject

8. Siblings <u>tend to bicker a lot</u>.
   a. simple predicate
   b. complete predicate

9. Mom and dad <u>bought</u> a new car.
   a. simple predicate
   b. complete predicate

10. Five years ago, we <u>moved to South Carolina</u>.
    a. simple subject
    b. complete subject
    c. simple predicate
    d. complete predicate

 Grammar Practice & Assess • imlovinlit.com

Name _____   Date _____

Lesson 2-2: Subject & Predicate Practice
Level B

C. Finding the Subject and Predicate

For each sentence, underline the subject or predicate listed in parentheses.

(11, complete predicate) In October, Carlos and his family moved to the United States from Mexico. (12, simple predicate) He was excited to go to his new school. (13, simple subject) He was going to be in Mrs. Jackson's class. (14, complete subject) Most of the kids were nice. (15, simple predicate) However, there was one kid who always gave him a hard time — Jacob.

(16, simple subject) Jacob didn't like Carlos because he looked different than the other kids in the class. (17, complete subject) The mean Jacob would call Carlos names. (18, complete predicate) He would make fun of the way that Carlos talked. (19, complete predicate) It bothered Carlos so much. (20, simple subject) Carlos knew he was different, but he didn't see why Jacob should make fun of him.

Instead of getting back at Jacob, Carlos did the right thing. He told an adult he knew would resolve the situation: his teacher. Mrs. Jackson took care of the problem and in the end, Jacob not only apologized to Carlos but also learned that he and Carlos had many things in common!

Name _____   Date _____

Lesson 2-2: Subject & Predicate Assessment

A. Recognizing Subjects and Predicates

Determine whether each statement describes the complete subject, simple subject, complete predicate, or simple predicate.

_____ 1. Uses one word that tells what the sentence is about

_____ 2. Uses multiple words that tell what the sentence is about

_____ 3. Uses an action or linking verb that tells what something does

_____ 4. Uses a verb and the words following it to tell what something does

a. complete subject
b. simple subject
c. complete predicate
d. simple predicate

B. Identifying Subjects and Predicates

Determine what the underlined portion of the sentence represents.

5. The beautiful <u>princess</u> married her charming prince.
   a. simple subject
   b. complete subject

6. Seven <u>dwarfs</u> helped the princess.
   a. simple subject
   b. complete subject

7. The enchanting prince <u>rode in on a white horse</u>.
   a. simple predicate
   b. complete predicate

8. He <u>gave</u> the princess a delicate kiss.
   a. simple predicate
   b. complete predicate

9. <u>Both the prince and the princess</u> lived happily ever after.
   a. simple subject
   b. complete subject

10. All of the elves, dwarfs, and creatures in the forest <u>waved</u> goodbye to them.
    a. simple subject
    b. complete subject
    c. simple predicate
    d. complete predicate

Lesson 2-2: Subject & Predicate Assessment

C. Finding the Subject and Predicate

For each sentence, underline the subject or predicate listed in parentheses.

(11, simple subject) When dogs lived in the wild, sometimes food was scarce.

(12, simple predicate) If they were able to find meat and bones, dogs became very protective

of it. (13, simple subject) Sometimes, they would have more meat than they could eat for one

meal. (14, complete predicate) To keep other dogs and animals from stealing their meat, dogs

would bury it in the ground. (15, complete predicate) When it was time for the next meal,

they would dig up their bones.

(16, complete subject) This game would continue until the meat and bones were gone.

(17, complete subject) Today, dogs' instincts still tell them to bury their bones and favorite

toys. (18, simple subject) They do this to keep other dogs and animals from stealing them!

(19, complete predicate) It was just like what their ancestors did. (20, complete subject)

Some dogs hide more than one bone at once. Even if dogs cannot bury their bones or other

"treasures" outside, they still have a tendency to find a secret spot for their special finds!

Name _____   Date _____

Lesson 2-3: Compound Subjects & Compound Predicates Practice

A. Recognizing Compound Subjects

Determine whether the underlined portion of the sentence is the compound subject or compound predicate and write **S**, **P**, or **N** (neither).

_____ 1. The <u>table and chairs</u> have been in our family for generations.
_____ 2. We <u>cleaned the living room and polished the floor</u>.
_____ 3. The <u>blue irises and yellow sunflowers</u> look beautiful in the garden.
_____ 4. The kids' meal came with <u>a hamburger and French fries</u>.
_____ 5. I <u>will play a game with you and cook dinner for you</u>.

B. Identifying Compound Subjects and Compound Predicates

For each number, write the letter of the sentence that corresponds to the given equation.

_____ 6. S + S + P
_____ 7. S + P + P
_____ 8. S + S + S + P
_____ 9. S + P + P + P
_____ 10. S + S + P + P

a. The cat, the dog, and the horse all walked along the road.
b. Mary and John play games together.
c. Sally likes reading books and loves watching movies.
d. Mom needs to go to the grocery store, do a load of laundry, and take me to practice.
e. Billy and Bob are twins and look exactly alike.

Lesson 2-3: Compound Subjects & Compound Predicates Practice
Level A

C. Applying Compound Subjects and Compound Predicates to Paragraphs
For each sentence, write the subject and predicate equation.

(11) The Dark Ages lasted from AD 410 to AD 710. (12) The British were ruling themselves and were not helped by the Romans. (13) The Saxons were fighting and trying to take over parts of Britain. (14) The Scots and the Picts were also fighting and taking over parts of the country. (15) The Dark Ages are also called Post-Roman times. (16) The Middle Saxon Times and Late Saxon Times followed the Dark Ages. (17) The empires and leaders created during the Dark Ages did not all last. (18) Foreign invaders would kidnap kids and have them work on their land. (19) Other crimes were very common. (20) The Dark Ages were indeed a very dark time.

11. _____   16. _____

12. _____   17. _____

13. _____   19. _____

14. _____   19. _____

15. _____   20. _____

Lesson 2-3: Compound Subjects & Compound Predicates Practice
Level B

A. Recognizing Compound Subjects

Determine whether the underlined portion of the sentence is the compound subject or compound predicate and write **S**, **P**, or **N** (neither).

_____ 1. <u>Berries and cherries</u> are my favorite fruits.

_____ 2. In the summer, <u>we have no homework and get to play outside</u>.

_____ 3. <u>Friday evening</u>, we went out for pizza.

_____ 4. <u>Monday, Tuesday, and Wednesday</u> are the slowest days of the week.

_____ 5. On Mondays, <u>I go to school and have a soccer game</u>.

B. Identifying Compound Subjects and Compound Predicates

For each number, write the letter of the sentence that corresponds to the given equation.

_____ 6. S + S + P

_____ 7. S + P + P

_____ 8. S + S + S + P

_____ 9. S + P + P + P

_____ 10. S + S + P + P

a. Jackson doesn't like reading, hates math, and has trouble writing.

b. Mrs. White sings the school song and reads the announcements.

c. Selena and Terry are going to the store and visiting the mall.

d. Washington and Oregon are on the West Coast.

e. Turkey, mashed potatoes, and stuffing are on the menu.

Lesson 2-3: Compound Subjects & Compound Predicates Practice
Level B

C. Applying Compound Subjects and Compound Predicates to Paragraphs
For each sentence, write the subject and predicate equation.

(11) In June, school lets out for summer! (12) Summer begins and brings lots of fun in the sun. (13) My bathing suit, sunscreen, and towel are all I need to have fun! (14) I head to the pool and chat with my friends. (15) Sarah, Jillian, and I absolutely love to swim and dive off the diving board. (16) At lunchtime, we usually take a break from the sun, go to Jillian's house, and play video games. (17) Later, we head back to the pool and soak up some more rays. (18) The girls and I wear lots of sunscreen and cover up well. (19) We definitely don't want sunburns! (20) Our summers are always so much fun.

11. _____

12. _____

13. _____

14. _____

15. _____

16. _____

17. _____

18. _____

19. _____

20. _____

Lesson 2-3: Compound Subjects & Compound Predicates Assessment

A. Recognizing Compound Subjects

Determine whether the underlined portion of the sentence is the compound subject or compound predicate and write **S**, **P**, or **N** (neither).

_____ 1. <u>My mom and my dad</u> spend a lot of time together.

_____ 2. On Friday, we <u>went to the movies and visited the nursing home</u>.

_____ 3. The <u>red and green</u> leaves looked beautiful.

_____ 4. <u>Six kittens and five puppies</u> were up for adoption at the shelter.

_____ 5. I <u>will call grandma and write her a letter</u> tonight.

B. Identifying Compound Subjects and Compound Predicates

Match each sentence with the correct sequence of subjects and predicates.

_____ 6. S + S + S + P

_____ 7. S + S + P + P

_____ 8. S + S + P + P + P

_____ 9. S + S + P

_____ 10. S + S + S + P + P

a. The Johnsons and the Murphys live together, go on vacation together, and spend a lot of time together.

b. My brother and my sister are my best friends and make me laugh.

c. Mexico and Canada border the United States.

d. Sarita, Jose, and Julio went out to eat.

e. The teacher, students, and principals helped set up the carnival and ran the carnival for the PTA.

Lesson 2-3: Compound Subjects & Compound Predicates Assessment

C. Applying Compound Subjects and Compound Predicates to Paragraphs
For each sentence, write the subject and predicate equation.

(11) My sister and I got to visit a real Hollywood movie set. (12) We saw actors and directors shooting scenes and acting on set. (13) Brad Park, Ryan Gregory, and George Carson were all there! (14) I called out to Brad Park and smiled at him. (15) He actually smiled back and waved right at me! (16) On the other hand, George Carson and Ryan Gregory ignored us and pretended not to see us! (17) My sister and I spent all day on the movie set, ate from the catering cart, and spotted even more movie stars. (18) At the end of the day, a director asked us to be extras in a movie and we got to go on an actual movie set! (19) Going on the set and being extras was so exciting! (20) I absolutely love Hollywood!

11. _____   16. _____

12. _____   17. _____

13. _____   18. _____

14. _____   19. _____

15. _____   20. _____

Grammar Practice & Assess • imlovinlit.com   **41**

Name _____ Date _____

Lesson 2-4: Simple & Compound Sentences Practice
Level A

A. Recognizing Simple and Compound Sentences

Determine whether each sentence is a simple or compound sentence and write **S** for simple and **C** for compound.

_____ 1. Jackson and James played baseball.

_____ 2. We went out to eat for Thanksgiving, but we stayed home for Christmas.

_____ 3. Pie is delicious.

_____ 4. Mom and Dad bought a new car.

_____ 5. I love school, but sometimes it can be boring.

B. Identifying Compound Sentences

Write the conjunction and/or punctuation mark that is used to turn each set of simple sentences into a compound sentence.

_____ 6. It was cold outside, so I wore my puffy coat.

_____ 7. Stella wanted a new phone, but she didn't have any money.

_____ 8. Joey made chocolate chip cookies, so I ate some.

_____ 9. Mom could bake cookies, or she could bake a cake.

_____ 10. It was snowing outside, and the sun was still shining.

C. Creating Compound Sentences

Write either a comma and a conjunction or a semicolon in each blank to turn each set of simple sentences into a compound sentence.

(11) During the Renaissance, Venice was known for its glass art _____ Milan was known for its iron. (12) Both were cities in Italy _____ both were very different. (13) Venice is known for its canals _____ Milan is known for its fashion. (14) Both cities are full of culture _____ they are popular tourist destinations. (15) Venice is pretty small _____ Milan is not much different in size. (16) You can travel from Venice to Milan _____ you might want to spend more than one day in each city. (17) Both cities have buildings and artifacts that were around during the Renaissance _____ they are full of history. (18) They both make good places to visit _____ they are educational too. (19) However, they are very different from the United States _____ make sure you plan ahead. (20) You might want to book a trip with a travel agency _____ you can do your research and book a trip yourself.

 Grammar Practice & Assess • imlovinlit.com   ©2015 Erin Cobb • CD-105007

Name _____   Date _____

Lesson 2-4: Simple & Compound Sentences Practice
Level B

A. Recognizing Simple and Compound Sentences
Determine whether each sentence is a simple or compound sentence and write **S** for simple and **C** for compound.

_____ 1. We went to the store.

_____ 2. We went to the pet store, but we didn't see any animals.

_____ 3. I like to eat cheese.

_____ 4. I want to play baseball in the summer, or I want to play soccer in the fall.

_____ 5. We threw away the turkey; it was raw in the middle.

B. Identifying Compound Sentences
Write the conjunction and/or punctuation mark that is used to turn each set of simple sentences into a compound sentence.

_____ 6. He did not understand his homework, so he did not do it.

_____ 7. I will buy a new car and I will sell my old car.

_____ 8. I want to go on the field, but I don't have enough money.

_____ 9. They went to the concert and they got to meet the band.

_____ 10. The snow was sparkly white; it was beautiful.

C. Creating Compound Sentences
Write either a comma and a conjunction or a semicolon in each blank to turn the simple sentences into a compound sentence. Write none if the sentence is not a compound sentence.

(11) There was a farmer _____ this farmer was a kind man who loved all creatures. (12) He would go out of his way _____ he would do whatever he could to make sure creatures were safe. (13) He made sure they were well-fed _____ he didn't care what kind of creature any of them were. (14) The farmer found a snake outside on the ground _____ it was cold. (15) It was freezing cold outside _____ there was snow on the ground. (16) The farmer felt sorry for the snake _____ he was shivering in the cold. (17) Ice was beginning to freeze on his scales. (18) The snake was known to be venomous _____ the farmer picked up the snake anyway. (19) He took him inside _____ he set the snake in front of the fire. (20) The snake became warm _____ he was ready to go back outside.

Name _____   Date _____

Lesson 2-4: Simple and Compound Sentences Assessment

A. Recognizing Simple and Compound Sentences

Determine whether each sentence is a simple or compound sentence and write **S** for simple and **C** for compound.

_____   1. The hockey game was exciting and the score was close.

_____   2. We're heading to North Dakota and South Dakota.

_____   3. I despise broccoli.

_____   4. We couldn't talk on the phone or we would get in trouble.

_____   5. I am smart.

B. Identifying Compound Sentences

Write the conjunction and/or punctuation mark that is used to turn each set of simple sentences into a compound sentence.

_____   6. I was sleepy, so I crawled into bed.

_____   7. I was angry, but I didn't tell him.

_____   8. Watching television is nice, but reading is better.

_____   9. Minivans are big and SUVs are cool.

_____   10. It was warm outside and I went swimming.

C. Creating Compound Sentences

Write either a comma and a conjunction or a semicolon in each blank to turn each set of simple sentences into a compound sentence.

(11) Everyone loved the violin _____ kings and queens enjoyed listening to it. (12) Street musicians played it _____ composers wrote music that featured it. (13) Orchestras quickly filled their seats with violinists _____ even more people wanted to play. (14) Everyone wanted a violin _____ Amati created a mold. (15) This allowed him to create many violins _____ still ensure each one had the same shape and quality as the original. (16) People played the violin _____ they were called violinists. (17) The violinist rested his chin on the chin rest _____ he held the neck of the violin in his hand. (18) He dragged a bow across the strings to make music _____ the bow was made of wood and horse hair. (19) The horse hair brushed across the strings _____ it caused them to vibrate. (20) The vibration was how the strings made music _____ it made a pleasant sound.

Name _____   Date _____

Lesson 2-5: Independent & Dependent Clauses Practice
Level A

A. Recognizing Independent and Dependent Clauses

Determine whether each sentence or fragment is an independent or dependent clause and write **D** (dependent) or **I** (independent).

_____ 1. After you write your name

_____ 2. I was in third grade.

_____ 3. Since you've been to France

_____ 4. Even if it is late

_____ 5. You're my best friend.

B. Forming Sentences with Independent and Dependent Clauses

Match each dependent clause with the appropriate independent clause.

_____ 6. You walk around the chairs

_____ 7. You failed the test

_____ 8. Bring your car into the garage

_____ 9. We will shake hands with the other team

_____ 10. There was a beautiful princess

a. Once upon a time

b. Even though you studied hard

c. Before the snow starts

d. While the music is playing

e. After the game ends

C. Analyzing Independent and Dependent Clauses

In each sentence, underline the dependent clause and circle the subordinate conjunction.

(11) Once I get home from school, I am going to do my homework. (12) I always do my homework first because it needs to be done. (13) After I do my homework, I will watch TV. (14) I prefer watching *Star Avengers*, even if *Judge Christopher* is also great. (15) I always watch TV, though sometimes my mom gives me chores to do. (16) Rather than do my chores, I make my little sister do them. (17) She always does them, unless she has lots of homework to do. (18) I pay her $3 a day to do my chores, as long as she does them well. (19) She says she deserves $5 a day, whereas I think that's too much. (20) Until she stops accepting the $3, I will continue paying her $3 a day.

Name _____   Date _____

A. Recognizing Independent and Dependent Clauses

Determine whether each sentence is an independent or dependent clause and write
D (dependent) or **I** (independent).

_____ 1. Because it was warm outside.

_____ 2. Unless it's midnight.

_____ 3. Even though I studied hard.

_____ 4. I don't like broccoli.

_____ 5. California is warm and sunny.

B. Forming Sentences with Independent and Dependent Clauses

Match each dependent clause with the appropriate independent clause.

_____ 6. I hide it under the table.

_____ 7. We'll go to the grocery store.

_____ 8. No one is happy.

_____ 9. He wore a winter coat.

_____ 10. Mrs. Johnson was happy to have a new last name.

a. Once we get there

b. Born Miss Marmalopolous

c. Even though it was sunny

d. If he isn't happy

e. Whenever she makes broccoli

C. Analyzing Independent and Dependent Clauses

In each sentence, underline the dependent clause and circle the subordinate conjunction.

(11) When Erica went off to college, she took along her favorite stuffed animal.
(12) Mr. Cuddles had been Erica's favorite since the day she was born. (13) Even though it wasn't cool to take a stuffed animal to school, Erica wanted him there. (14) Going to college was crazy, even with Mr. Cuddles. (15) She sat Mr. Cuddles on her bed, even though others could see him. (16) Whenever kids came to her room, she'd introduce them. (17) Erica loved Mr. Cuddles, because he was special. (18) However, after going to class one day, Erica returned to find Mr. Cuddles was gone! (19) Erica didn't know what she'd do if she didn't have Mr. Cuddles. (20) Erica was a wreck until she found Mr. Cuddles under the bed.

Name _____   Date _____

Lesson 2-5: Independent & Dependent Clauses Assessment

A. Recognizing Independent and Dependent Clauses

Determine whether each sentence is an independent or dependent clause and write **D** (dependent) or **I** (independent).

_____ 1. After we eat.
_____ 2. I like eating bacon and eggs.
_____ 3. Since I turned eight.
_____ 4. No matter what you say.
_____ 5. I need a new car.

B. Forming Sentences with Independent and Dependent Clauses

Match each dependent clause with the appropriate independent clause.

_____ 6. We left for vacation.
_____ 7. We got in an accident.
_____ 8. I'll get started on the project.
_____ 9. The piper left the town.
_____ 10. We get to go sledding.

a. Five days ago
b. When it snows
c. Unless you have a better idea
d. On the way to the store
e. Playing a happy song

C. Analyzing Independent and Dependent Clauses

In each sentence, underline the dependent clause and circle the subordinate conjunction.

(11) As long as people could remember, the town of Hamlin was infested by rats. (12) Even though the townspeople tried, they couldn't get rid of them. (13) The rats crawled in the houses and filled the streets until they were full! (14) The people didn't know what to do since nothing worked. (15) Although they tried everything, the rats were still there. (16) The rats drove them crazy until a piper came to town. (17) Whether he knew what he was doing or not, the piper had a magical effect on the rats. (18) Whenever he played his pipe, the rats followed him. (19) They followed him until he stopped. (20) They followed him up and down the streets until one day, they followed him right out of town!

Name _____   Date _____

Lesson 2-6: Sentences, Fragments, & Run-Ons Practice

A. Defining Sentences, Fragments, and Run-Ons
Match each statement with the type of sentence it defines.

_____ 1. Not a complete thought

_____ 2. Has the proper amount of subjects and predicates

_____ 3. Can seem confusing or lengthy

    a. fragment

    b. run-on

    c. sentence

B. Identifying Sentences, Fragments, and Run-Ons
Decide whether each statement is a sentence (S), fragment (F), or run-on (RO).

_____ 4. Once upon a time.

_____ 5. George and Anna rode their bikes.

_____ 6. Mom and Dad went on a date they went to a new restaurant.

_____ 7. I will be 12 on my next birthday it will be December 10.

_____ 8. I just don't get it.

_____ 9. Run-on sentences seem to go on and on even though they are often short sometimes they don't make sense.

_____ 10. When the dinosaurs roamed the planet.

C. Labeling Sentences, Fragments, and Run-Ons
For each sentence, write **S** for sentence, **F** for fragment, or **RO** for run-on.

(11) Every year on my birthday. (12) My family takes me out to breakfast, and then we head to my favorite store on Earth so I can pick out a birthday present. (13) I like getting to pick out my own present my family always buys things I don't like. (14) When I pick out my own present. (15) I can get exactly what I want. (16) This year, I want a new bike. (17) My old bike has a broken tire that makes it difficult to ride. (18) It makes a clicking sound when I pedal and sometimes it locks up and sometimes it gets squeaky and sometimes it's no fun. (19) My new bike will be red. (20) It will have white and yellow stripes.

11. _____

12. _____

13. _____

14. _____

15. _____

16. _____

17. _____

18. _____

19. _____

20. _____

Lesson 2-6: Sentences, Fragments, & Run-Ons Assessment

A. Defining Sentences, Fragments, and Run-Ons

Match each statement with the type of sentence it defines.

_____ 1. Could be a dependent clause

_____ 2. Needs punctuation

_____ 3. Missing the completion of a thought

_____ 4. Is a complete thought

_____ 5. Stands alone

a. sentence

b. run-on

c. fragment

B. Identifying Sentences, Fragments, and Run-Ons

Decide whether each statement is a sentence (S), fragment (F), or run-on (RO).

_____ 6. Last Monday morning, it snowed.

_____ 7. Two weeks ago.

_____ 8. My sister likes cats and hates dogs.

_____ 9. Maybe tomorrow we can go to the store do we need hot dogs.

_____ 10. How often do you?

C. Labeling Sentences, Fragments, and Run-Ons

For each sentence, write **S** for sentence, **F** for fragment, or **RO** for run-on.

(11) Once upon a time. (12) There was a man. (13) He lived thousands of years ago we only have a faint idea of what he looked like. (14) In fact, we do not know very much about him at all. (15) What we do know about the man. (16) We have learned from what we have found deep in the ancient soil. (17) Archaeologists have dug up artifacts and have traveled through dark caves. (18) They have come up with drawings, skeletons, and other items that have helped us learn a little more about that man who was that man? (19) He was the great-great-grandfather of the human race. (20) From what we know, he looked nothing like most humans look today.

11. _____

12. _____

13. _____

14. _____

15. _____

16. _____

17. _____

18. _____

19. _____

20. _____

Name _____   Date _____

Lesson 3-1: Common & Proper Nouns Practice

A. Describing Common and Proper Nouns
Determine whether each definition describes common (C) or proper (P) nouns.

_____ 1. Normally special names for nouns
_____ 2. Typically begin with capital letters
_____ 3. Just regular people, places, and things
_____ 4. Names for specific things

B. Labeling Common and Proper Nouns
Label each noun as common (C) or proper (P).

_____ 5. doctor   _____ 8. Mr. Oakes
_____ 6. highway   _____ 9. honesty
_____ 7. Highway 9   _____ 10. mom

C. Identifying Common and Proper Nouns in Paragraphs
Circle the noun or nouns in each sentence. Then, write whether each noun is common or proper. Do not circle pronouns.

(11) The Temple in Ancient Greece was decorated with sculptures and paintings (12) from famous artists who donated their time. (13) One of the most famous sculptures was a statue of Jupiter. (14) It was carved from ivory and accented with jewels. (15) The gardens of the Temple were also full of statues. (16) When an athlete won one of the games, (17) a sculptor was commissioned to create a life-size statue. (18) Those statues filled the Temple's gardens. (19) Athletics were not the only talents on display during the Olympics. (20) Interestingly, musicians and poets competed as well.

11. _____   16. _____
12. _____   17. _____
13. _____   18. _____
14. _____   19. _____
15. _____   20. _____

Name _____   Date _____

Lesson 3-1: Common & Proper Nouns Assessment

A. Describing Common and Proper Nouns
Determine whether each definition describes common (C) or proper (P) nouns.

_____ 1. Very specific

_____ 2. Regular enough to be in the dictionary

_____ 3. Don't usually start with a capital letter

B. Labeling Common and Proper Nouns
Label each noun as common (C) or proper (P).

_____ 4. Governor Johnson   _____ 8. secretary

_____ 5. oven   _____ 9. Burger Queen

_____ 6. comforter   _____ 10. The Bill of Rights

_____ 7. Antarctica

C. Identifying Common and Proper Nouns in Paragraphs
Circle the noun or nouns in each sentence. Then, write whether each noun is common or proper. Do not circle pronouns.

(11) The Greek god, Hercules, was not only known for his strength. (12) He was also known for his athletic prowess. (13) To encourage people to visit the temple at Olympia, (14) Hercules held many athletic events. (15) These included spear throwing, wrestling, boxing and chariot races. (16) Hercules was the umpire for the games and would award a crown of olive leaves to the winner. (17) During the games, one group of people stood out. (18) They were called the Spartans (19) and they were known for being great athletes. (20) Not surprisingly, they won the majority of the awards during the Olympics.

11. _____   16. _____

12. _____   17. _____

13. _____   17. _____

14. _____   19. _____

15. _____   20. _____

Name _____   Date _____

Lesson 3-2: Concrete & Abstract Nouns Practice

A. Defining Concrete and Abstract Nouns

Determine whether each statement describes a concrete (C) or abstract (A) noun.

_____ 1. Can see with your eyes

_____ 2. Concepts and ideas

_____ 3. Regular nouns

_____ 4. You cannot use your five senses to find them

B. Identifying Concrete and Abstract Nouns

Identify each noun as concrete (C) or abstract (A).

_____ 5. berry

_____ 6. fire

_____ 7. bravery

_____ 8. frustration

_____ 9. dishonesty

_____ 10. puppy

C. Analyzing Common and Abstract Nouns

In each sentence, circle the common nouns and underline the abstract nouns. Then, write your explanation. Do not circle pronouns.

(11) I like to look at the clouds. (12) Clouds bring about calmness. (13) They float by dreamily in the sky. (14) I like to imagine that I see different shapes in the clouds. (15) I see knights and ogres. (16) I also see soldiers fighting for peace (17) and heroes known for their strength. (18) The clouds fuel my imagination! (19) They give me ideas for my stories. (20) The clouds are silent inspirations.

11. _____

12. _____

13. _____

14. _____

15. _____

16. _____

17. _____

18. _____

19. _____

20. _____

Name _____   Date _____

Lesson 3-2: Concrete & Abstract Nouns Assessment

A. Defining Concrete and Abstract Nouns

Determine whether each statement describes a concrete (C) or abstract (A) noun.

_____ 1. You can "touch" it.   _____ 3. It is regular

_____ 2. You cannot "touch" it.   _____ 4. It is a concept

B. Identifying Concrete and Abstract Nouns

Identify each noun as concrete (C) or abstract (A).

_____ 5. sadness   _____ 8. hamburger

_____ 6. honor   _____ 9. ecosystem

_____ 7. cousin   _____ 10. honesty

C. Analyzing Common and Abstract Nouns

In each sentence, circle the common nouns and underline the abstract nouns. Then, write your explanation.

(11) The little girl's imagination is incredible. (12) The stories in her mind (13) are full of beauty and adventure. (14) She imagines dragons and fairies. (15) They feast on mushrooms and flowers. (16) They dance jigs and climb mountains. (17) They are known for their energy and creativity. (18) She imagines animals and princesses. (19) They live in forests and castles, (20) but mostly they live in her dreams.

11. _____

12. _____

13. _____

14. _____

15. _____

16. _____

17. _____

18. _____

19. _____

20. _____

Name _____   Date _____

Lesson 3-3: Plural Nouns Practice

A. Recognizing Plural Nouns

Match each plural with its rule.

_____ 1. salads   a. When a word ends with *s, ss, ch, sh, x,* or *z*: add *-es*

_____ 2. berries   b. When a word ends with *f* or *fe*: change *f* to *v* and add *-es*

_____ 3. shelves   c. When a word ends with *us*: change *us* to *i*

_____ 4. nuclei   d. When a word ends with a consonant + *y*: change *y* to *i* and add *-es*

_____ 5. identities   e. With most nouns, just add *s*

B. Identifying Plural Nouns

Choose the correct plural for each noun.

_____ 6. rich
   a. richs
   b. richi
   c. richis
   d. riches

_____ 7. fungus
   a. fungi
   b. fungal
   c. fungus'
   d. funguss

_____ 8. artillery
   a. artillerys
   b. artilleries
   c. artilleri
   d. artilleris

_____ 9. hero
   a. heros
   b. heros'
   c. heroes
   d. hero

_____ 10. pass
   a. passes
   b. passus
   c. passi
   d. pass'

C. Writing Plural Nouns

Write the plural form of each noun in parentheses.

On Halloween, (11) _____ (witch) and (12) _____ (goblin) fill the

(13) _____ (street). They are filling their (14) _____ (bag) with

(15) _____ (candy) as they go door-to-door begging for (16) _____ (treat).

At the stroke of midnight, the sound of (17) _____ (wolf) usher them back inside

where they survey their (18) _____ (treasure) from the (19) _____

(festivity) of the night. Then, they head to their (20) _____ (bed) and say good night.

Lesson 3-3: Plural Nouns Assessment

A. Recognizing Plural Nouns

Match each plural with its rule.

_____ 1. crosses

_____ 2. knives

_____ 3. crunches

_____ 4. syllabi

_____ 5. cherries

a. When a word ends with *s*, *ss*, *ch*, *sh*, *x*, or *z*: add *-es*

b. When a word ends with *f* or *fe*: change *f* to *v* and add *-es*

c. When a word ends with *us*: change *us* to *i*

d. When a word ends with a consonant + *y*: change *y* to *i* and add *-es*

B. Identifying Plural Nouns

Choose the correct plural for each noun.

_____ 6. itch
  a. itchis
  b. itches
  c. itchs
  d. itchus

_____ 7. scarf
  a. scarves
  b. scarfes
  c. scarvis
  d. scarfs

_____ 8. life
  a. lives
  b. lifes
  c. lifs
  d. livs

_____ 9. bookshelf
  a. bookshelfs
  b. bookshelves
  c. bookshelfes
  d. bookshelves

_____ 10. firefly
  a. fireflys
  b. firefly
  c. fireflies
  d. fireflyes

C. Writing Plural Nouns

Write the plural form of each noun in parentheses.

"Are you (11) _____ (man) or (12) _____ (mouse)?" asked the chief. "What does that mean?" the (13) _____ (soldier) shouted back. "It means, are you timid little (14) _____ , (boy) or are you (15) _____ (warrior)?" the chief shouted back. "We are (16) _____ (fighter)," shouted the soldiers. They were all new (17) _____ (recruit) ready to risk their (18) _____ (life) for their (19) _____ (country), even if that meant losing their (20) _____ (identity) in the process.

Name _____   Date _____

Lesson 3-4: Possessive Nouns Practice

A. Understanding Possessive Nouns
Write the letter that tells what you need to do to form the possessive form of each noun.

_____ 1. dogs
_____ 2. door
_____ 3. John and Sarah (not together)
_____ 4. Mom and dad (together)

a. Add an 's
b. Add an '
c. Add an 's after the last noun
d. Add an 's after each noun

B. Identifying Possessive Nouns
Choose the correctly formed possessive noun.

_____ 5. trees
a. trees'
b. tree's
c. trees
d. trees's

_____ 6. siblings
a. siblings
b. sibling's
c. siblings'
d. sib'lings

_____ 7. Friday
a. Friday's
b. Fridays
c. Friday'
d. Fridays'

_____ 8. hunter
a. hunters
b. hunter's
c. hunters'
d. hunters's

_____ 9. bed
a. beds
b. bed's
c. beds'
d. beds's

_____ 10. Jack and Olivia (not together)
a. Jack and Olivia's
b. Jack's and Olivia's
c. Jacks and Olivia's
d. Jacks and Olivias'

C. Forming Possessive Nouns
Write the possessive form of each noun in parentheses.

(11) Tonight, we're going to _____ (Sarah, Jackie, and Alex) houses for a progressive dinner. (12) That is when you go to different _____ (people) houses for separate courses of a meal. (13) We'll go to _____ (Sarah) for appetizers, (14) _____ (Jackie) house for dinner, (15) and _____ (Alex) for dessert. (16) The _____ (girls) houses are nearby, (17) so we don't need my _____ (mom and dad) car. (18) We'll walk on our _____ (neighborhood) new sidewalk. (19) We'll obey the _____ (crosswalks) signs too. (20) When we arrive at the first house, we'll enjoy our _____ (friend) part of the meal.

Name _____   Date _____

Lesson 3-4: Possessive Nouns Assessment

A. Understanding Possessive Nouns
Write the letter that tells what you need to do to form the possessive form of each noun.

_____ 1. people

_____ 2. cats

_____ 3. friend

_____ 4. Grandma and Grandpa

a. Add an 's

b. Add an '

c. Add an 's after the last noun

d. Add an 's after each noun

B. Identifying Possessive Nouns
Choose the correctly formed possessive noun.

_____ 5. mothers
- a. mothers'
- b. mother's
- c. mothers
- d. mothers's

_____ 6. vultures
- a. vultures'
- b. vulture's
- c. vultures
- d. vultures's

_____ 7. chariot
- a. chariots
- b. chariots'
- c. chariot's
- d. chariots's

_____ 8. mom and pop
- a. mom's and pop's
- b. mom and pop's
- c. moms and pops'
- d. mom and pops'

_____ 9. countries
- a. country's
- b. countries'
- c. countrie's
- d. countries's

_____ 10. men
- a. mens
- b. mens'
- c. men's
- d. mens's

C. Forming Possessive Nouns
Write the possessive form of each noun in parentheses.

(11) The Ancient _____ (Egyptians) writing used symbols called hieroglyphics. (12) "Hieroglyphics" is Egyptian for "_____ (god) words." (13) They used symbols for letters. The letter _____ (A) symbol was a bird. and (14) _____ (L) symbol was a lion. (15) _____ (archaeologists) theories about hieroglyphics came from pyramid walls. (16) The _____ (pyramids) wall had messages about the people buried there. (17) They told about _____ (kings) lives (18) and other _____ (royalty) stories. (19) Today, _____ (people) versions of hieroglyphics don't mean as much as (20) the Ancient _____ (Egyptians) versions.

Lesson 4-1: Action, Linking, & Helping Verbs Practice
Level A

A. Understanding Action, Linking, and Helping Verbs
Decide whether each statement describes an action (A), linking (L), or helping (H) verb.

_____   1. Related to an action

_____   2. Related to a state of being

_____   3. Related to helping the action

B. Identifying Action, Linking, and Helping Verbs
Decide whether each verb is an action (A), linking (L), or helping (H) verb.

_____   4. catch   _____   8. feel

_____   5. be   _____   9. are

_____   6. should   _____   10. give

_____   7. talk

C. Labeling Action, Linking, and Helping Verbs
Underline the verb(s) in each sentence. Then, write whether the verb(s) you underlined are action, linking, or helping verbs.

(11) Tomorrow, I am running a race! (12) It is my first cross country race. (13) I will run five miles along the course. (14) Yesterday, I was nervous. (15) Today, I am excited! (16) I looked at the other runners' times. (17) My personal best is better than theirs. (18) I hope I can win this race. (19) It will take a lot of determination. (20) I feel confident in myself!

11. _____   16. _____

12. _____   17. _____

13. _____   18. _____

14. _____   19. _____

15. _____   20. _____

Name _____   Date _____

Lesson 4-1: Action, Linking, & Helping Verbs Practice
Level B

A. Understanding Action, Linking, and Helping Verbs
Decide whether each statement describes an action (A), linking (L), or helping (H) verb.

_____ 1. Expresses an action

_____ 2. Shows a state of being

_____ 3. Helps the main verb express an action

B. Identifying Action, Linking, and Helping Verbs
Decide whether each verb is an action (A), linking (L), or helping (H) verb.

_____ 4. jump   _____ 8. draw

_____ 5. shall   _____ 9. taste

_____ 6. frustrate   _____ 10. being

_____ 7. seem

C. Labeling Action, Linking, and Helping Verbs
Underline the verb(s) in each sentence. Then, write whether the verb(s) you underlined are action, linking, or helping verbs.

(11) I must go to the store. (12) We are out of bacon, eggs, and bread. (13) We eat bacon, eggs, and bread every morning. (14) Maybe I can go to the store early in the morning. (15) The store opens at 5 a.m. and (16) the rest of my family gets up at 6 a.m. (17) So, I will return before they get up. (18) I feel less stressed, (19) but now I am hungry. (20) I can hear the bacon sizzling already!

11. _____   16. _____

12. _____   17. _____

13. _____   18. _____

14. _____   19. _____

15. _____   20. _____

Name _____   Date _____

Lesson 4-1: Action, Linking, & Helping Verbs Assessment

A. Understanding Action, Linking, and Helping Verbs

Decide whether each statement describes an action (A), linking (L), or helping (H) verb.

_____   1. It's an expression of an action.
_____   2. It works with the main verb to express an action.
_____   3. It involves a state of being.

B. Identifying Action, Linking, and Helping Verbs

Decide whether each verb is an action (A), linking (L), or helping (H) verb.

_____   4. look   _____   8. fight
_____   5. sound   _____   9. could
_____   6. must   _____ 10. been
_____   7. drive

C. Labeling Action, Linking, and Helping Verbs

Underline the verb(s) in each sentence. Then, write whether the verb(s) you underlined are action, linking, or helping verbs.

(11) I am going to pass this class! (12) I study hard every night. (13) Also, I complete all my homework. (14) Usually, I get good grades on all my tests. (15) So why am I worried? (16) This class is hard and (17) it takes a lot of work. (18) I feel overwhelmed. (19) It seems like a sure thing, (20) but I will keep working hard—just in case.

11. _____   16. _____
12. _____   17. _____
13. _____   18. _____
14. _____   19. _____
15. _____   20. _____

Name _____   Date _____

Lesson 4-2: Predicate Nominatives & Predicate Adjectives Practice
Level A

A. Recognizing Predicate Nominatives and Predicate Adjectives

Determine if the underlined word is a predicate nominative (PN) or predicate adjective (PA).

_____   1. Yesterday was <u>Sunday</u>.

_____   2. The weather is <u>windy</u>.

_____   3. My mom looks <u>pretty</u>.

_____   4. Sam seems <u>upset</u>.

_____   5. Chocolate is <u>yummy</u>.

B. Identifying Predicate Nominatives and Predicate Adjectives

Write the predicate nominative or predicate adjective in each sentence on the line. Next to each word, write whether it is a predicate nominative (PN) or predicate adjective (PA).

6. My brother is very mean.   _____   _____

7. Mark became a doctor.   _____   _____

8. Sean looks mad.   _____   _____

9. Turkeys are plump.   _____   _____

10. Mark is a suspect in the case.   _____   _____

Lesson 4-2: Predicate Nominatives & Predicate Adjectives Practice
Level A

C. Writing Predicate Nominatives and Predicate Adjectives
On the table, write the subject, linking verb, and noun or adjective for each sentence. If there is no linking verb, write **NLV**.

(11) John was a smart kid. (12) He was a hard worker. (13) He was determined. (14) As a result, John became an astronaut. (15) He is a good astronaut. (16) John has been my hero for years. (17) He is such a nice guy. (18) Right now, John is in space. (19) He will remain in space for one year. (20) One day, I will become an astronaut like John.

	Subject	Linking Verb	Noun or Adjective
11.			
12.			
13.			
14.			
15.			
16.			
17.			
18.			
19.			
20.			

Lesson 4-2: Predicate Nominatives & Predicate Adjectives Practice
Level B

A. Recognizing Predicate Nominatives and Predicate Adjectives

Circle the predicate nominative or predicate adjective in each sentence on the line. Then, write whether it is a predicate nominative (PN), predicate adjective (PA), or neither (NE).

_____ 1. Our town is known as the best place to live in the Midwest.

_____ 2. The cat feels just like soft yarn.

_____ 3. The rose bush grew quickly.

_____ 4. People are interested in planning a fundraiser for the tornado victims.

_____ 5. Cheering for my favorite team is fun.

B. Identifying Predicate Nominatives and Predicate Adjectives

Divide each sentence to show the subject, linking verb, and noun or adjective. Note in parentheses whether the final word is a noun or adjective.

6. Friends are wonderful people to have in your life.

_____

7. Dogs seem happy when they are around humans.

_____

8. Scarlet does not seem scared of ghosts at night.

_____

9. Rudolph's nose becomes red when he flies.

_____

10. Purple irises smell beautiful in the spring.

_____

Lesson 4-2: Predicate Nominatives & Predicate Adjectives Practice
Level B

C. Writing Predicate Nominatives and Predicate Adjectives

Underline the predicate nominatives and predicate adjectives. Write them on the corresponding lines below and note whether each word is a predicate nominative (PN) or predicate adjective (PA).

(11) Have you ever read the story of Frankenstein? It is a book about a monster. (12) Mary Shelley is the author who wrote the book Frankenstein. (13) Frankenstein is a monster created by a scientist. (14) He resembles a zombie. (15) In the story, Frankenstein is a murderer. (16) However, he feels bad about the murder. (17) He felt angry, and (18) he felt lonely. (19) So, he committed the murder. The scientist is not compassionate. (20) He refuses to make a companion for Frankenstein. So Frankenstein commits another murder and runs away. The scientist is the murderer in the eyes of the law.

11. _____   _____

12. _____   _____

13. _____   _____

14. _____   _____

15. _____   _____

16. _____   _____

17. _____   _____

18. _____   _____

19. _____   _____

20. _____   _____

Name _____   Date _____

Lesson 4-2: Predicate Nominatives & Predicate Adjectives Assessment

A. Recognizing Predicate Nominatives and Predicate Adjectives

Circle the predicate nominative or predicate adjective in each sentence on the line. Then, write whether it is a predicate nominative (PN), predicate adjective (PA), or neither (NE).

_____ 1. The cake tastes delicious when it is warm.

_____ 2. My fever grew hotter during the night.

_____ 3. Veronica is a graceful dancer, particularly when she dances ballet.

_____ 4. The yellow shirt doesn't fit him properly.

_____ 5. The scientist's discovery represents a breakthrough in elemental science.

B. Identifying Predicate Nominatives and Predicate Adjectives

Divide each sentence to show the subject, linking verb, and noun or adjective. Note in parentheses whether the final word is a noun or adjective.

6. Her father became a rich man when he won the lottery.

_____

7. The woman's face became concerned when her dog ran off.

_____

8. The footsteps grew louder as they came closer.

_____

9. I feel like a generous person around the holidays.

_____

10. My sisters are incredibly difficult people to communicate with.

_____

Lesson 4-2: Predicate Nominatives & Predicate Adjectives Assessment

C. Writing Predicate Nominatives and Predicate Adjectives

Underline the predicate nominatives and predicate adjectives. Write them on the corresponding lines below and note whether each word is a predicate nominative (PN) or predicate adjective (PA).

(11) Helium is the second element on the periodic table. (12) It is also the second most abundant element in the universe. (13) A French astronomer first discovered Helium on the sun. The year was 1868. (14) The astronomer saw a yellow line by the sun. It seemed odd. (15) The sun is a ball of gas, but the scientist did not recognize the gas in the line. (16) Helium was responsible for that line. (17) That's how helium got its name. Helios is the sun god. (18) Helium is a form of the name Helios. (19) Helium is a noble gas. (20) It is simple, but it does a lot of things. For example, it makes balloons float and helps scuba divers breathe underwater.

11. _____   _____
12. _____   _____
13. _____   _____
14. _____   _____
15. _____   _____
16. _____   _____
17. _____   _____
18. _____   _____
19. _____   _____
20. _____   _____

Lesson 4-3: Past, Present, & Future Perfect Tense Practice

A. Understanding Tenses

Match each tense with its definition.

a. present tense
b. present perfect tense
c. past tense

d. past perfect tense
e. future tense
f. future perfect tense

_____ 1. Something that has already happened
_____ 2. Something that will have ended before a specific time or event in the future
_____ 3. Something that happened before another past action or state of being
_____ 4. Something that is happening now
_____ 5. Something that will happen
_____ 6. Something that began in the past and may still be going on

B. Identifying Tenses

Identify the tense of each sentence.

_____ 7. She writes.
  a. present tense
  b. past tense
  c. future tense
  d. present perfect tense

_____ 8. She ate yesterday.
  a. present tense
  b. past tense
  c. future tense
  d. present perfect tense

_____ 9. She had played yesterday.
  a. present tense
  b. past tense
  c. future tense
  d. past perfect tense

_____ 10. She will go next week.
  a. present tense
  b. past tense
  c. future tense
  d. future perfect tense

Name _____   Date _____

Lesson 4-3: Past, Present, & Future Perfect Tense Practice

C. Labeling Sentences by Tense

Label each sentence or clause with the correct tense.

(11) My mom works for Mr. Johnson. (12) This March, she will have worked for Mr. Johnson for fifteen years. (13) In the past, my mom has gotten a bonus on the anniversary of her hire. (14) She hopes to receive one this year, too. (15) Maybe this year's bonus will be bigger than last year's. (16) I hope so. (17) Mr. Johnson called my mom into his office yesterday. (18) He told her she was a good worker. (19) He has been impressed with her work, so (20) that is a good sign!

11. _____

12. _____

13. _____

14. _____

15. _____

16. _____

17. _____

18. _____

19. _____

20. _____

Name _____   Date _____

Lesson 4-3: Past, Present, & Future Perfect Tense Assessment

A. Understanding Tenses

Match each tense with its description.

a. present tense   d. past perfect tense
b. present perfect tense   e. future tense
c. past tense   f. future perfect tense

_____ 1. If it has a singular subject, add -s.
_____ 2. It is formed with helping verb had.
_____ 3. It is formed by adding -ed.
_____ 4. It is formed with helping verbs will or shall.
_____ 5. It is formed with helping verbs will have or shall have.
_____ 6. It is formed with helping verbs has or have.

B. Identifying Tenses

Identify the tense of each sentence.

_____ 7. Margo has walked today.
a. present tense
b. past tense
c. future tense
d. present perfect tense

_____ 9. Margo had walked yesterday.
a. present tense
b. past tense
c. future tense
d. past perfect tense

_____ 8. Margo walked today.
a. present tense
b. past tense
c. future tense
d. past perfect tense

_____ 10. Margo will walk tomorrow.
a. present tense
b. past tense
c. future tense
d. future perfect tense

Lesson 4-3: Past, Present, & Future Perfect Tense Assessment

C. Labeling Sentences by Tense

Label each sentence or clause with the correct tense.

(11) Today, mom is taking me to the store. (12) She has taken me to the store on this day for five years. (13) We go school shopping on the same day every year. (14) Last year, we went school shopping with my older sister. (15) This year, my older sister wanted to go shopping by herself. (16) We are sad that she doesn't want to come with us, (17) but we will have fun without her. (18) I am excited about our shopping trip. (19) By the end of this shopping trip, my legs will be worn out, (20) but I will be the most fashionable kid at school!

11. _____   16. _____

12. _____   17. _____

13. _____   18. _____

14. _____   19. _____

15. _____   20. _____

Name _____   Date _____

Lesson 4-4: Infinitives & Participles Practice
Level A

A. Understanding Infinitives and Participles
Match the part of the verb with its definition.

_____ 1. Add the helping verb *is*   a. infinitive
_____ 2. Base form of the verb   b. present participle
_____ 3. Add *-ed*, in most cases   c. past
_____ 4. Add *have* and *-ed*   d. past participle

B. Identifying Principal Parts
Identify the principal part of the verb.

_____ 5. Sherry is tallying the scores.   a. infinitive
_____ 6. I tallied the scores.   b. present participle
_____ 7. She wants to tally the score.   c. past
_____ 8. She has tallied the scores.   d. past participle

C. Changing Principal Parts
Identify the verb tense used in each sentence.

(9) Sarah likes to gaze at the stars in the evening. (10) She has gazed at the stars for years. (11) I know why she likes to gaze at the stars. (12) She is imagining that the stars represent wishes. (13) Once, she imagined that all her wishes came true. (14) She has wished for many things. (15) One night, she wished for a pony. (16) The next day, a pony showed up at her house. (17) Tonight she is wishing for something else. (18) I like to gaze at the stars with her. (19) Some nights, I try to make a wish too. (20) I want to wish for Sarah's wish to come true.

9. _____   15. _____
10. _____   16. _____
11. _____   17. _____
12. _____   18. _____
13. _____   19. _____
14. _____   20. _____

Name _____   Date _____

Lesson 4-4: Infinitives & Participles Practice

A. Understanding Infinitives and Participles

Match the part of the verb with its definition.

_____ 1. Something started in the past that continues   a. infinitive

_____ 2. Something that was a previous action   b. present participle

_____ 3. Something that is continuous   c. past

_____ 4. The base form   d. past participle

B. Identifying Principal Parts

Identify the principal part of the verb.

_____ 5. I am riding a bike.   a. infinitive

_____ 6. I rode a bike.   b. present participle

_____ 7. I always love to ride my bike.   c. past

_____ 8. I have ridden a bike.   d. past participle

C. Changing Principal Parts

Write the correct form of each verb based on the principal part listed in parentheses.

(9) We _____ (go, present participle) to my grandma's house. (10) We _____ (go, past participle) every week for the last three months. (11) In fact, we just _____ (go, past) last week. (12) I like _____(visit, infinitive) my grandma. (13) We _____(visit, present participle) her so often (14) because she _____ (feel, present participle) lonely. (15) All of her family members _____ (live, present participle) far away, (16) so we _____ (drive, present participle) to visit her often. (17) I _____ (wish, present participle) we could move closer. (18) We _____ (move, past) away last year. (19) My dad _____ (have, past) a new job, (20) so we _____ (lived, past participle) far away since then.

Name _____   Date _____

Lesson 4-4: Infinitives & Participles Assessment

A. Understanding Infinitives and Participles
Match the part of the verb with its definition.

_____ 1. Adds the verb *is*   a. infinitive
_____ 2. Is the base form of the verb   b. present participle
_____ 3. Adds -*ed* to the end   c. past
_____ 4. Adds *have* and -*ed* to the end   d. past participle

B. Identifying Principal Parts
Identify the principal part of the verb.

_____ 5. She has rung the bell.   a. infinitive
_____ 6. She is ringing the bell.   b. present participle
_____ 7. She rang the bell.   c. past
_____ 8. She tries to ring the bell.   d. past participle

C. Changing Principal Parts
Write the correct form of each verb based on the principal part listed in parentheses.

(9) I'm so glad we _____ (come, past) to dinner. (10) Now, let's try _____
(pay, infinitive) the bill quickly. (11) Who _____ (pay, present participle) the
bill tonight? (12) I _____ (pay, past) the bill last time. (13) Sarah _____ (pay,
past participle) the bill in the past. (14) Jessica, I guess it is your turn to _____ (pay,
infinitive) the bill. (15) We _____ (order, past) four pizzas and _____
(drink, past) three pitchers of soda. (16) That is more soda than we _____
(drink, past participle) in the past. (17) I guess we _____ (drink, present participle)
more soda each week. (18) We _____ (eat, present participle) less pizza though,
so it all evens out. (19) We _____ (meet, present participle) here at the same time
next week. (20) We _____ (meet, past participle) here at the same time every week
for two months.

Lesson 4-5: Direct & Indirect Objects Practice
Level A

A. Describing Direct and Indirect Objects

Decide whether each description names a direct (DO) or indirect (IO) object.

_____ 1. Who receives the action

_____ 2. Who is affected by the action

_____ 3. Answers question such as for whom? or whom?

_____ 4. Answers questions such as who? or what?

B. Identifying Direct and Indirect Objects

Identify each underlined word as the direct object (DO), indirect object (IO), or neither (N).

_____ 5. I gave <u>my sister</u> a present.

_____ 6. The doctor wrote <u>me</u> a prescription.

_____ 7. President Coolidge read a <u>prepared statement</u> to the citizens.

_____ 8. Mrs. Coolidge wrote letters for <u>them</u>.

_____ 9. <u>President Coolidge</u> gave a speech on TV.

_____ 10. My mother <u>needs</u> to buy herself a new pair of shoes.

C. Labeling Direct and Indirect Objects

Label the direct and indirect objects in each sentence by writing **DO** or **IO** over each one. Note: Not every sentence will have an indirect object.

(11) I sent my mom a postcard from Florida. (12) My mom sent me a postcard back. (13) My postcard had a picture of sunshine on it. (14) Her postcard had a picture of snow on it. (15) My mom was going to build a snowman for me. (16) I was going to build a sandcastle for my mom. (17) We were both going to build something for each other. (18) She sent me a shovel for the sandcastle. (19) I sent her a scarf for the snowman. (20) We enjoy the correspondence.

Lesson 4-5: Direct & Indirect Objects Practice
Level B

A. Describing Direct and Indirect Objects

Decide whether each description names a direct (DO) or indirect (IO) object.

_____ 1. The receiver of the action

_____ 2. Someone or something affected by the action

_____ 3. Answers the question *Whom?* or *For whom?*

_____ 4. Answers the question *Who?* or *What?*

B. Identifying Direct and Indirect Objects

Identify each underlined word as the direct object (DO), indirect object (IO), or neither (N).

_____ 5. My dad is a <u>funny</u> guy.

_____ 6. I do not like my sister's <u>boyfriend</u>.

_____ 7. He gave <u>the kids</u> a bath.

_____ 8. I took the <u>package</u> to the post office.

_____ 9. We sent a present to my <u>grandma</u>.

_____ 10. That is <u>my brother's</u> dog.

C. Labeling Direct and Indirect Objects

Label the direct and indirect objects in each sentence by writing **DO** or **IO** over each one. Note: Not every sentence will have an indirect object.

(11) Our principal presented us with a surprise. (12) He was giving our teachers a break.

(13) He was sending the teachers to the spa! (14) We would get to have a party. (15) We went

to the gym. (16) A DJ took requests from the students. (17) Waiters served the students snacks.

(18) There were fun games. (19) There were no teachers. (20) We sent our thanks to the

principal.

Name _____   Date _____

Lesson 4-5: Direct & Indirect Objects Assessment

A. Describing Direct and Indirect Objects

Decide whether each description names a direct (DO) or indirect (IO) object.

_____   1. A person receiving the action
_____   2. A person affected by the action
_____   3. A person that represents *Whom?*
_____   4. A person that represents *Who?*

B. Identifying Direct and Indirect Objects

Identify each underlined word as the direct object (DO), indirect object (IO), or neither (N).

_____   5. I bought <u>my sister</u> a pony.
_____   6. Jason gave <u>him</u> ten dollars.
_____   7. Won't you tell us your <u>secret</u>?
_____   8. Please give this message to your <u>mother</u>.
_____   9. No, I won't take <u>you</u> to the fair.
_____   10. The <u>circus</u> is her favorite place.

C. Labeling Direct and Indirect Objects

Label the direct and indirect objects in each sentence by writing **DO** or **IO** over each one.
Note: Not every sentence will have an indirect object.

(11) The waiter brought us the bill. (12) My father forgot his wallet. (13) My mother passed

him her wallet. (14) He took out the credit card. (15) He gave the bill and card to the waiter.

(16) We left the restaurant. (17) My dad handed me the keys. (18) I drove the car to our house.

(19) On the way, I got a speeding ticket. (20) The cop handed the ticket to my dad.

Name _____   Date _____

Lesson 5-1: Prepositions Practice

A. Understanding Prepositions

Match each preposition with its role.

_____ 1. throughout   a. when
_____ 2. upon   b. where
_____ 3. since   c. how
_____ 4. beside   d. why
_____ 5. about

B. Identifying Prepositions

Identify the preposition in each sentence.

_____ 6. You should get a letter at 10:00 a.m. tomorrow.

_____ 7. The wind is heading toward the house.

_____ 8. The ship is sailing between the two islands.

_____ 9. I will meet you at 9:00 a.m.

_____ 10. Please turn in your paper by 9:00 p.m.

C. Analyzing Prepositions

Circle the preposition in each sentence and write whether it tells **where**, **why**, **when**, or **how**.

(11) When you go outside your house, (12) look above you. (13) Despite the city lights, (14) you will see thousands of twinkling lights up in the sky. (15) The lights shine every night, even behind the clouds. (16) They are found underneath the moon (17) and beyond the horizon. (18) They shine down on Earth (19) and make you feel as if you are standing beneath a magic blanket. (20) If you see a star shooting across the sky, make a wish!

11. _____
12. _____
13. _____
14. _____
15. _____
16. _____
17. _____
18. _____
19. _____
20. _____

Name _____   Date _____

Lesson 5-1: Prepositions Practice

Level B

A. Understanding Prepositions
Match each preposition with its role.

_____ 1. during   a. when
_____ 2. after   b. where
_____ 3. above   c. how
_____ 4. because of   d. why
_____ 5. with

B. Identifying Prepositions
Identify the preposition in each sentence.

_____ 6. The puppy is in the box.
_____ 7. We will meet you at school.
_____ 8. I found my earring among the clover.
_____ 9. My sister hasn't been home since December.
_____ 10. I can do the dishes without my mom's help.

C. Analyzing Prepositions
Circle the preposition in each sentence and write whether it tells **where**, **why**, **when**, or **how**.

(11) Here is a little caterpillar on the leaf! (12) He is stuffing his stomach with lots of food. (13) He grows bigger and bigger until he makes a cocoon. (14) His cocoon hangs from the branch. (15) Sometimes, it sways in the breeze. (16) The caterpillar is transforming into a butterfly. (17) All of the transformation takes place inside the cocoon. (18) When he breaks out of the cocoon, he will be a beautiful butterfly. (19) I can't wait for him to emerge from the cocoon (20) and fly through the air!

11. _____   16. _____
12. _____   17. _____
13. _____   18. _____
14. _____   19. _____
15. _____   20. _____

Lesson 5-1: Prepositions Assessment

A. Understanding Prepositions

Match each preposition with its role.

_____ 1. past

_____ 2. because of

_____ 3. below

_____ 4. with

_____ 5. after

a. when

b. where

c. how

d. why

B. Identifying Prepositions

Identify the preposition in each sentence.

_____ 6. I'm from Ohio.

_____ 7. I'd like a bag of apples.

_____ 8. My cat likes to walk along the fence.

_____ 9. Have a seat on the couch.

_____ 10. I'll meet you inside the restaurant.

C. Analyzing Prepositions

Circle the preposition in each sentence and write whether it tells **where**, **why**, **when**, or **how**.

(11) Have you ever flown in a plane? (12) Tomorrow, I am going to fly across the country. (13) I have never been inside an airport before, (14) and this will be my first time on an airplane. (15) The plane will climb up (16) and fly through the air. (17) I will be sure to study the safety manual before takeoff! (18) That way, I will know what to expect while we are in the air. (19) I wonder if I will be allowed to walk about the plane. (20) Maybe I will even get to go in the cockpit.

11. _____

12. _____

13. _____

14. _____

15. _____

16. _____

17. _____

18. _____

19. _____

20. _____

Name _____   Date _____

Lesson 5-2: Prepositional Phrases Practice

A. Understanding Prepositional Phrases

Decide whether each description names the preposition (P), prepositional phrase (PP), or the object of the preposition (O).

_____ 1. Describes when, where, why, and how

_____ 2. Has both a preposition and a noun

_____ 3. Only has a noun

B. Identifying Prepositional Phrases

Underline the prepositional phrase in each sentence.

4. The plane flew above the clouds.
5. Turkeys want to fly below the radar.
6. I have been awake for most of the night.
7. It's no fun to go to the mall too early in the morning.
8. We will take our tree down after the holiday.
9. My dad kissed my mom beneath the mistletoe.
10. Jack stood against the wall.

C. Analyzing Prepositional Phrases

Underline the prepositional phrase(s) in each sentence and write the object of the preposition.

(11) Every year, we hang holiday lights on our porch. (12) We put red lights on the first column. (13) We put green lights around the second column. (14) We place a snowman sleeve over the porch light. (15) We hang a wreath beneath the porch light. (16) We also add multi-colored lights to the bushes below the porch. (17) My dad places mistletoe above the front door. (18) He likes to give my mom a kiss under the mistletoe. (19) We can't walk through the door until he gives her a kiss. (20) It wouldn't be the holidays without the decorations!

11. _____

12. _____

13. _____

14. _____

15. _____

16. _____

17. _____

18. _____

19. _____

20. _____

Name _____   Date _____

Lesson 5-2: Prepositional Phrases Practice
Level B

A. Understanding Prepositional Phrases

Decide whether each description names the preposition (P), prepositional phrase (PP), or the object of the preposition (O).

_____ 1. Starts with a preposition

_____ 2. Is a noun

_____ 3. A single word that usually starts the phrase

B. Identifying Prepositional Phrases

Underline the prepositional phrase in each sentence.

4. We bought cookies at the bakery.

5. I'm sure I'll find my keys somewhere around the house.

6. No, the grocery store is past the bank.

7. You'll find our hideout if you go through the woods.

8. We're headed over the river to grandmother's house.

9. I haven't been there since 1993.

10. We're going sledding down the hill.

C. Analyzing Prepositional Phrases

Underline the prepositional phrase(s) in each sentence and write the object of the preposition.

(11) My favorite place is found deep in the woods. (12) To get there, you must walk along the river. (13) The path meandered between the trees. (14) Then, you walk across the river. (15) You turn right by the old oak tree. (16) After that, you crawl under the bushes. (17) My favorite place is inside the last bush. (18) It is quiet under that bush. (19) No one can hear me in that place. (20) I can sit and be alone with my thoughts.

11. _____   16. _____

12. _____   17. _____

13. _____   18. _____

14. _____   19. _____

15. _____   20. _____

Name _____   Date _____

Lesson 5-2: Prepositional Phrases Assessment

A. Understanding Prepositional Phrases

Decide whether each description names the preposition (P), prepositional phrase (PP), or the object of the preposition (O).

_____   1. When, where, why, how

_____   2. Incorporates a preposition and a noun

_____   3. A noun

B. Identifying Prepositional Phrases

Underline the prepositional phrase in each sentence.

4. The bus drove across town.

5. I put the book in my backpack.

6. We went out for pizza after the game.

7. They rode horses along the beach.

8. I forgot to pick my sister up from school.

9. It's warm and cozy under my fleece blanket.

10. My favorite restaurant is down the street.

C. Analyzing Prepositional Phrases

Underline the prepositional phrase(s) in each sentence and write the object of the preposition.

(11) Every year, we travel to my grandpa's beach house in North Carolina. (12) We usually go during the summer, (13) but some years we also go in the spring. (14) I love to go down to North Carolina. (15) The sunrise is beautiful on the beach. (16) My feet feel warm in the sand. (17) The fish in the water tickle my toes. (18) I like to watch the boats on the water (19) and walk across the dunes. (20) I can't wait until we go to my grandpa's beach house this year!

11. _____   16. _____

12. _____   17. _____

13. _____   18. _____

14. _____   19. _____

15. _____   20. _____

Lesson 5-3: Adverb Phrases & Adjective Phrases Practice
Level A

A. Describing Adverb and Adjective Phrases
Determine whether each description describes an adverb (ADV) or adjective (ADJ) phrase.

_____ 1. When?

_____ 2. Which one?

_____ 3. Where?

_____ 4. How much?

_____ 5. How many?

B. Identifying Adverb and Adjective Phrases
Underline the adverb or adjective phrase in each sentence.

6. We need to buy a carton of milk.

7. My dad fixed the car with his tools.

8. Tomorrow morning, we are going to the grocery store.

9. Every Monday is a fun Monday.

10. Jonathan wishes he could play with the toys.

C. Analyzing Adverb and Adjective Phrases
For each sentence, underline any adverb or adjective phrases and write the part of speech being modified.

(11) I chased a rabbit down the street. (12) It was a fast rabbit with white feet. (13) My cat tried to catch the cute little rabbit in the bushes. (14) I had to hold my cat in my arms to stop him. (15) He wanted to play with the rabbit. (16) If I let him, he would probably want to eat the rabbit for his dinner. (17) This was not a good fate for the rabbit. (18) Tomorrow morning, I am going to lock up my cat. (19) He will stay in the house. (20) Of course, he will stay there all day long.

11. _____

12. _____

13. _____

14. _____

15. _____

16. _____

17. _____

18. _____

19. _____

20. _____

Lesson 5-3: Adverb Phrases & Adjective Phrases Practice
Level B

A. Describing Adverb and Adjective Phrases
Determine whether each description describes an adverb (ADV) or adjective (ADJ) phrase.

_____ 1. Describes what kind

_____ 2. Describes how often

_____ 3. Describes how many

_____ 4. Describes when

_____ 5. Describes to what extent

B. Identifying Adverb and Adjective Phrases
Underline the adverb or adjective phrase in each sentence.

6. I have a bag of candy.

7. We met everybody at the airport.

8. My sister does her chores without care.

9. Alicia ran with great speed.

10. The apples fell on the ground.

C. Analyzing Adverb and Adjective Phrases
For each sentence, underline the adverb or adjective phrase and write the part of speech being modified.

(11) My grandmother is a woman with a big heart. (12) She also is a woman of great wisdom. (13) I don't ever visit her without learning something new. (14) She graduated from Harvard University, (15) but she says her knowledge came from life experience. (16) Whenever I need advice, I go to my grandma's house. (17) She even lets me visit at night. (18) She's also available in the early morning. (19) She tries to help me with my problems. (20) She is a grandmother with lots of love.

11. _____   16. _____

12. _____   17. _____

13. _____   18. _____

14. _____   19. _____

15. _____   20. _____

Lesson 5-3: Adverb Phrases & Adjective Phrases Assessment

A. Describing Adverb and Adjective Phrases

Determine whether each description describes an adverb (ADV) or adjective (ADJ) phrase.

_____ 1. Modifies a noun

_____ 2. Modifies an adverb

_____ 3. Modifies a pronoun

_____ 4. Modifies a verb

_____ 5. Modifies an adjective

B. Identifying Adverb and Adjective Phrases

Underline the adverb or adjective phrase in each sentence.

6. This is a jar of pickles.

7. She met someone on the train.

8. He liked to run late at night.

9. She eats every morning.

10. Joel is angry with his father.

C. Analyzing Adverb and Adjective Phrases

For each sentence, underline any adverb or adjective phrases and write the part of speech being modified.

(11) This is a box of old coins. (12) It was given to me by my father. (13) It was given to him by his father. (14) I keep the box on the shelf. (15) The shelf sits above my bed. (16) I like to take it out in the morning (17) and look at all the coins in the box. (18) There are coins from everywhere around the world. (19) My dad said my grandpa collected most of them during the war. (20) My dad used to look at them late at night.

11. _____

12. _____

13. _____

14. _____

15. _____

16. _____

17. _____

18. _____

19. _____

20. _____

Name _____   Date _____

Lesson 6-1: Pronouns Practice

Level A

A. Describing Pronoun Types
Match each type of pronoun with the phrase that best describes it.

_____ 1. Relates the verb back to the subject   a. personal pronouns

_____ 2. Not specific   b. possessive pronouns

_____ 3. Helps understand ownership   c. indefinite pronouns

_____ 4. Takes the place of subject or object   d. demonstrative pronouns

_____ 5. Used with questions   e. reflexive pronouns

_____ 6. Relates to something specific   f. interrogative pronouns

B. Identifying Pronouns
Circle the pronoun in each sentence.

7. Are those the kind you wanted?   9. Did you get one for yourself?

8. Our puppy is so cute.   10. Whose idea was that?

C. Identifying Types of Pronouns
Circle each pronoun. Write the type of pronoun it represents.

(11) Are you sure you want to buy those? (12) I saw a
story about them on the news. (13–14) It said they were
known to break. (15–16) You don't believe me?
(17–18) You can watch the news story and decide for
yourself. (19–20) I'm just glad they'll be yours and
not mine!

11. _____

12. _____

13. _____

14. _____

15. _____

16. _____

17. _____

18. _____

19. _____

20. _____

Name _____   Date _____

Lesson 6-1: Pronouns Practice

A. Describing Pronoun Types

Match each type of pronoun with the phrase that best describes it.

_____ 1. Helps direct the action of the verb
_____ 2. Is used to show ownership
_____ 3. Is not specific
_____ 4. Helps ask a question
_____ 5. Points out something specific
_____ 6. Your typical pronouns

a. Personal pronouns
b. Possessive pronouns
c. Indefinite pronouns
d. Demonstrative pronouns
e. Reflexive pronouns
f. Interrogative pronouns

B. Identifying Pronouns

Circle the pronoun in each sentence.

7. Vivian doesn't like anyone.

8. This is going to be a good day.

9. She bought herself a new pair of shoes.

10. He got those for somebody else.

C. Identifying Types of Pronouns

Circle each pronoun. Write the type of pronoun it represents.

(11) Have you figured out (12) who was responsible for vandalizing the cars? (13) I would've

tried to (14) figure it out (15) myself, but (16) you have more resources. (17) I hope (18) you

can figure (19) this out before (20) something else is damaged!

11. _____
12. _____
13. _____
14. _____
15. _____

16. _____
17. _____
18. _____
19. _____
20. _____

Name _____   Date _____

Lesson 6-1: Pronouns Assessment

A. Describing Pronoun Types

Match each type of pronoun with the phrase that best describes it.

_____ 1. Directs the action of the verb back to the subject   a. whom

_____ 2. Does not refer to any specific person, place, thing, or amount   b. her

_____ 3. Shows ownership   c. some

_____ 4. Replaces the subject or object   d. these

_____ 5. Used to ask questions   e. herself

_____ 6. Points out a specific person, place, thing, or idea   f. him

B. Identifying Pronouns

Circle the pronoun in each sentence.

7. To whom do I owe the honor?

8. That shoe belongs to me.

9. I will get it myself.

10. What are you talking about?

C. Identifying Types of Pronouns

Circle each pronoun. Write the type of pronoun it represents.

(11) This is going to be a great day. (12) I woke up on the right side of the bed. (13) I made (14) myself a delicious breakfast. Then, (15) my mom drove me to school and (16) we got there early! (17) My crush was waiting for (18) me at the door. (19) He was holding a bouquet with (20) several of the flowers from his garden.

11. _____   16. _____

12. _____   17. _____

13. _____   18. _____

14. _____   19. _____

15. _____   20. _____

Lesson 6-2: Identifying Pronoun Types Practice
Level A

A. Matching Pronouns
Match each pronoun with the correct sentence.

_____ 1. They gave us _____ of the ketchup packets
to go with our meal.

_____ 2. _____ is my favorite.

_____ 3. _____ shoes hurt my feet.

_____ 4. He only has _____ to thank.

_____ 5. I'm not sure _____ it was.

a. himself
b. whose
c. these
d. several
e. yours

B. Identifying Pronouns
Circle the pronoun in each sentence and select its type.

_____ 6. He doesn't want to talk about the trip.

_____ 7. The shoes that belong to him are red and white.

_____ 8. His picture is hanging on the wall in the hallway.

_____ 9. What can Bonnie do to get herself into college?

_____ 10. To whom does the bag belong?

a. personal pronoun
b. demonstrative pronoun
c. indefinite pronoun
d. reflexive pronoun
e. possessive pronoun
f. interrogative pronoun

C. Using Pronouns
Complete each sentence with the proper pronoun.

(11) _____ chips are delicious! (12) When he told me they were _____

favorite, (13) I didn't believe _____ . (14) Now that I've tried _____,

(15) I think _____ (16) are _____ favorite too. (17) I'll have to get some for

_____ and (18) maybe I'll get some for _____ too. (19) I won't get any for

_____ siblings though. (20) They'll have to get some for _____ .

Lesson 6-2: Identifying Pronoun Types Practice
Level B

A. Matching Pronouns

Match each pronoun with the correct sentence.

_____ 1. I'm old enough to stay home by _____ .

_____ 2. _____ aren't for you.

_____ 3. We're headed to _____ house for the holidays.

_____ 4. _____ wants to help me.

_____ 5. Can you tell me _____ of the trains to take?

a. myself
b. which
c. those
d. nobody
e. their

B. Identifying Pronouns

Circle the pronoun in each sentence and select its type.

_____ 6. Give yourselves plenty of time to get to the airport.

_____ 7. Could you ask somebody to help me?

_____ 8. He is an incredibly nice person.

_____ 9. What do you have on your list?

_____ 10. I am very tired.

a. personal pronoun
b. demonstrative pronoun
c. indefinite pronoun
d. reflexive pronoun
e. possessive pronoun
f. interrogative pronoun

C. Using Pronouns

Complete each sentence with the proper pronoun.

(11) My mom wants to know _____ (interrogative pronoun) is on

(12) _____ (possessive pronoun) birthday list. (13) _____ (personal

pronoun, objective) told (14) _____ (personal pronoun, objective) that I hadn't

made (15) _____ (personal pronoun, subjective) yet. (16) I don't think I want

_____ (indefinite pronoun) for my birthday. (17) Instead, I would like to get

_____ (indefinite pronoun) for (18) _____ (indefinite pronoun) else.

(19) I wonder _____ (interrogative pronoun) I could get (20) _____

(indefinite pronoun) for.

Lesson 6-2: Identifying Pronoun Types Assessment

A. Matching Pronouns

Match each pronoun with the correct sentence.

_____ 1. There are _____ of my photo albums in the attic.		a. himself
_____ 2. _____ is the house you were going to?		b. whose
_____ 3. I believe this mess is _____ .		c. these
_____ 4. Peter decided he wanted to keep the presents for _____ .		d. several
_____ 5. I'll take _____ .		e. yours

B. Identifying Pronouns

Circle the pronoun in each sentence and select its type.

_____ 6. Those are your responsibility.	a. personal pronoun
_____ 7. His is the one that is broken.	b. demonstrative pronoun
_____ 8. Why don't you ask him yourself?	c. indefinite pronoun
_____ 9. Who does that belong to?	d. reflexive pronoun
_____ 10. How old is he?	e. possessive pronoun
	f. interrogative pronoun

C. Using Pronouns

Complete each sentence with the proper pronoun.

(11) Amy is _____ (possessive pronoun) best friend. (12) _____ (personal pronoun, subjective) have been best friends for five years. (13) I first met _____ (personal pronoun, objective) when (14) _____ (personal pronoun, subjective) moved in next door. (15) _____ (personal pronoun, subjective) do (16) _____ (indefinite pronoun) together. (17) Usually, Amy and _____ (personal pronoun, subjective) find (18) _____ (reflexive pronoun) laughing hysterically when we're together. (19) _____ (indefinite pronoun) else seems to find (20)_____ (possessive pronoun) jokes funny, but we do.

Name _____   Date _____

Lesson 7-1: Kinds of Adjectives Practice

A. Understanding Adjectives
Match each description with the kind of adjective it describes.

_____ 1. Tend to be short   a. describers
_____ 2. Related to proper nouns   b. demonstrative adjectives
_____ 3. Regular adjectives   c. proper adjectives
_____ 4. Point out something specific   d. articles

B. Identifying Adjectives
Match each adjective with the kind of adjective it represents.

_____ 5. a   a. describers
_____ 6. orange   b. demonstrative adjectives
_____ 7. angry   c. proper adjectives
_____ 8. Greek   d. articles
_____ 9. horrid
_____10. these

C. Labeling Adjectives
Label each adjective as a **describer**, **demonstrative adjective**, **proper adjective**, or **article**.

(11) My dad is French and German. (12) He likes to say he is European. (13) Where this description comes from, I don't know. (14) After all, my dad is American. (15) My ancestors who came from Germany and France were European. (16) They were also rich, (17) but they came to America on a large boat (18) and spent a lot of their money (19) in the process. (20) That was a poor decision in my opinion.

11. _____   16. _____
12. _____   17. _____
13. _____   18. _____
14. _____   19. _____
15. _____   20. _____

Lesson 7-1: Kinds of Adjectives Practice
Level B

A. Understanding Adjectives
Match each description with the kind of adjective it describes.

_____ 1. Typically very short words
_____ 2. Typically capitalized
_____ 3. Typical adjectives
_____ 4. Typically note a particular thing or group

a. describers
b. demonstrative adjectives
c. proper adjectives
d. articles

B. Identifying Adjectives
Match each adjective with the kind of adjective it represents.

_____ 5. that
_____ 6. an
_____ 7. ferocious
_____ 8. Alaskan
_____ 9. horrible
_____10. these

a. describers
b. demonstrative adjectives
c. proper adjectives
d. articles

C. Labeling Adjectives
Label each underlined adjective as a **describer, demonstrative adjective, proper adjective,** or **article.**

(11) This year for my elective, I am taking (12) an (13) African dance class. I think African dance is (14) exciting. I also like other types of dance, particularly (15) Irish dance and (16) Russian ballet. (17) Those (18) Russian ballet dancers are very (19) disciplined, while African dancers are more (20) carefree.

11. _____
12. _____
13. _____
14. _____
15. _____

16. _____
17. _____
18. _____
19. _____
20. _____

Name _____   Date _____

Lesson 7-1: Kinds of Adjectives Assessment

A. Understanding Adjectives

Match each description with the kind of adjective it describes.

_____ 1. Name something specific

_____ 2. Represent the majority of adjectives

_____ 3. Are usually very basic and short words

_____ 4. Usually start with capital letters

a. describers

b. demonstrative adjectives

c. proper adjectives

d. articles

B. Identifying Adjectives

Match each adjective with the kind of adjective it represents.

_____ 5. Japanese

_____ 6. a

_____ 7. that

_____ 8. foreign

_____ 9. former

_____ 10. adorable

a. describers

b. demonstrative adjectives

c. proper adjectives

d. articles

C. Labeling Adjectives

Label each underlined adjective as a **describer**, **demonstrative adjective**, **proper adjective**, or **article**.

Have you ever heard of McRay Investments? (11) <u>That</u> company has experienced (12) <u>incredible</u> growth this year. It started out as (13) <u>a</u> (14) <u>small</u> company with its (15) <u>former</u> CEO, Jim Johnson. With its (16) <u>new</u> CEO, it has done <u>amazing</u> things. The (17) <u>latter</u> CEO has instituted a lot of new policies. (18) <u>Those</u> have helped cut down on costs and get rid of (19) <u>lazy</u> workers. (20) Now, McRay Investments is <u>an</u> awesome company to work for.

11. _____

12. _____

13. _____

14. _____

15. _____

16. _____

17. _____

18. _____

19. _____

20. _____

Lesson 7-2: Degrees of Comparison Practice

A. Describing Degrees of Comparison

Match each word with the way to form its comparative and superlative forms.

_____ 1. most adorable
_____ 2. brighter
_____ 3. crazier

a. one-syllable words: add -er or -est
b. two-syllable words: add -er or -est or more or most
c. three or more syllable words: add more or most

B. Identifying Degrees of Comparison

Identify whether each word or phrase is written using the positive (P), comparative (C), or superlative (S) form.

_____ 4. longer
_____ 5. most insignificant
_____ 6. more disgusting
_____ 7. politest

_____ 8. more reasonable
_____ 9. furthest
_____ 10. most youthful

C. Using Degrees of Comparison

Follow the descriptions in parentheses to form the correct degree of comparison for each word.

(11) Today has been the _____ (bad, superlative) day of my life. (12) It started off when my alarm clock went off _____ (late, comparative) than it was supposed to. (13) Then my shower was _____ (cold, comparative) than it was supposed to be. (14) My mom also served the _____ (nasty, superlative) oatmeal for breakfast. (15) Then I went to the bus stop and found out that my bus had come _____ (early, comparative) than it usually does, (16) so I had to walk to school even though it felt like the _____ (cold, superlative) day of the year. (17) When I got to school, my _____ (good, superlative) friend (18) decided she'd found a _____ (good, comparative) group of friends to hang out with. (19) I had to eat lunch all by myself and it was the _____ (lonely, superlative) part of my day. (20) I don't think tomorrow can be _____ (bad, comparative) than today.

Name _____   Date _____

Lesson 7-2: Degrees of Comparison Assessment

A. Describing Degrees of Comparison

Match each word with the way to form its comparative and superlative forms.

_____ 1. crazy (comparative)

_____ 2. agreeable (superlative)

_____ 3. tired (comparative)

a. Add *more*

b. Add *-er*

c. Add *most*

B. Identifying Degrees of Comparison

Identify whether each word or phrase is written using the positive (P), comparative (C), or superlative (S) form.

_____ 4. most unusual

_____ 5. uglier

_____ 6. laziest

_____ 7. pricey

_____ 8. more functional

_____ 9. easiest

_____ 10. tallest

C. Using Degrees of Comparison

Follow the descriptions in parentheses to form the correct degree of comparison for each word.

(11) This year I have been asked to sing a solo for our school's first choir concert. I am going to be the _____ (good, superlative) soloist the school has ever had. (12) When I sing my solo, it will be _____ (clear, comparative) than anything I have sung before (13) and my voice will be the _____ (loud, superlative) on stage. (14) The microphone I'm wearing will make me sound even _____ (loud, comparative). (15) My choir instructor said my voice was the _____ (beautiful, superlative) voice she had ever heard. (16) She said it was even _____ (beautiful, comparative) than the voice of a professional singer. (17) I think that was the _____ (nice, superlative) compliment anyone has ever given me! (18) She is also the _____ (good, superlative) music teacher I have ever had, even _____ (good, comparative) than last year's music teacher. (20) I can't wait for this concert because it is going to be the _____ (awesome, superlative) performance I have ever given.

Lesson 8-1: Adverbs Practice

Level A

A. Describing Adverbs

Match each adverb with the question it answers.

_____ 1. over
_____ 2. last week
_____ 3. fast
_____ 4. too
_____ 5. sometimes

a. How?
b. When?
c. Where?
d. How long?
e. To what extent?

B. Identifying Adverbs

Underline the adverb in each sentence.

6. The treasure is here.
7. Jessica acted quickly when she heard the alarm.
8. Lyssa occasionally attends choir practice.
9. My brother is asleep in the bed below.
10. We're going on vacation next week.

C. Labeling Adverbs

Underline the adverb in each sentence. Then, write the purpose of the adverb.

(11) Truthfully, I don't like swimming. (12) I tell my parents I like it, but I honestly don't like it. (13) So why do I lie to them? Because I know swimming is really important to them. (14) It's not like I'm very good at it, though. (15) They simply just want to see me swim. (16) I think that's amazingly wonderful, (17) but I still hate it. (18) I wonder if my parents would be completely supportive if I told them the truth. (19) I absolutely can't keep on doing something I hate, (20) so I guess I really have no choice but to tell them.

11. _____
12. _____
13. _____
14. _____
15. _____

16. _____
17. _____
18. _____
19. _____
20. _____

Lesson 8-1: Adverbs Practice

Level B

A. Describing Adverbs

Match each adverb with the question it answers.

_____ 1. frequently   a. How?
_____ 2. backwards   b. When?
_____ 3. gracefully   c. Where?
_____ 4. later   d. How long?
_____ 5. greatly   e. To what extent?

B. Identifying Adverbs

Underline the adverb in each sentence.

6. Chompers, my dog, always greets me enthusiastically.

7. She balanced her books precariously on the edge of her desk.

8. He seldom goes to the store unless he is really hungry.

9. I am utterly disappointed by your very rude behavior.

10. He was taking the kids upstairs.

C. Labeling Adverbs

Underline the adverb in each sentence. Then, write **manner**, **place**, **time**, or **degree** to tell the purpose of the adverb.

(11) We never do anything fun as a family. (12) My parents work late. (13) When they get home, they are usually tired. (14) If I ask them to go anywhere, they say they are too tired. (15) On the weekend, we always have errands to run. (16) Just once, I would like to forget the errands. (17) It would be really fun to go see a movie or go on a hike. (18) It can even be someplace nearby. (19) Doing things as a family is very important, (20) but my parents totally don't understand.

11. _____   16. _____
12. _____   17. _____
13. _____   18. _____
14. _____   19. _____
15. _____   20. _____

Name _____   Date _____

Lesson 8-1: Adverbs Assessment

A. Describing Adverbs

Match each adverb with the question it answers.

_____	1. easily	a.	How?
_____	2. there	b.	When?
_____	3. today	c.	Where?
_____	4. seldom	d.	How long?
_____	5. too	e.	To what extent?

B. Identifying Adverbs

Underline the adverb in each sentence.

6. She is walking here, there, and everywhere.

7. Amal clearly doesn't want to be here.

8. He turned in near the gas station.

9. The Board of Directors holds its meeting annually.

10. Yesterday, she proudly sang the Star-Spangled Banner.

C. Labeling Adverbs

Underline the adverb in each sentence. Then, write **manner**, **place**, **time**, or **degree** to tell the purpose of the adverb.

(11) The cheerleaders loudly cheered on the football team (12) as they quickly ran out of the locker room. (13) They did the same thing every week. (14) Sometimes, they carried a banner (15) for the football players to excitedly break through. (16) Often, fans came on to the field to cheer with them. (17) Football games are really fun for the cheerleaders. (18) They don't get too tired, (19) even though they're cheering energetically during the game. (20) Many of them would do it daily if they could.

11. _____

12. _____

13. _____

14. _____

15. _____

16. _____

17. _____

18. _____

19. _____

20. _____

Lesson 8-2: More Adverb Phrases Practice
Level A

A. Describing Adverb Phrases
Decide whether each description of an adverb phrase is true (T) or false (F).

_____ 1. A phrase can begin with the word *with*.

_____ 2. A phrase cannot begin with the word *without*.

_____ 3. A phrase can begin with the word *love*.

_____ 4. A phrase can begin with the word *on*.

_____ 5. A phrase with *like* or *as* is a simile.

B. Recognizing Adverb Phrases
Decide whether each sentence contains an adverb phrase. Write yes (Y) or no (N).

_____ 6. This cake is as fluffy as a cloud.

_____ 7. We're baking a strawberry cake with real strawberries.

_____ 8. Please don't add mayonnaise to the chicken salad.

_____ 9. Never drive a car without a licensed driver.

_____ 10. I love my sister, who is the only family I have.

C. Identifying Adverb Phrases
Underline the adverb phrase in each sentence.

(11) I like to eat my cereal with bananas. (12) I put the bananas in before the milk. (13) I put the milk in last, since I like to drench the bananas. (14) The bananas look delicious in the bowl. (15) But, they look even more delicious on my spoon, (16) and they taste even more delicious in my mouth! (17) I hardly ever eat cereal without bananas. (18) Come to think of it, I put bananas in my cereal every day! (19) It started about a few months back, but (20) now it happens on a regular basis.

Name _____   Date _____

Lesson 8-2: More Adverb Phrases Practice
Level B

A. Describing Adverb Phrases

Decide whether each description of an adverb phrase is true (T) or false (F).

_____ 1. An adverb phrase relates to manner.

_____ 2. An adverb phrase asks a question.

_____ 3. An adverb phrase only modifies a noun.

_____ 4. An adverb phrase relates to time.

_____ 5. An adverb phrase can show frequency.

B. Recognizing Adverb Phrases

Decide whether each sentence contains an adverb phrase. Write yes (Y) or no (N).

_____ 6. He made a hole with the drill.

_____ 7. You must do your homework before dinnertime.

_____ 8. Jonathan gets a new magazine in the mail every month.

_____ 9. Before you watch TV, you need to finish your chores.

_____ 10. I really like your sweater.

C. Identifying Adverb Phrases

Underline the adverb phrase in each sentence.

(11) Every single month, Amanda wants to go to the store. (12) She wants to go to the store to buy new clothes. (13) She also likes to buy clothes for her sisters (14) and she buys them with her own money. (15) Erica works ten hours every week. (16) She saves the money from her paychecks. (17) She always gets paid on Friday. (18) At the end of the month, she looks at her bank statement to see how much she earned. (19) She knows that's the money she can use to go shopping. (20) She usually has a lot of money to buy clothes.

Lesson 8-2: More Adverb Phrases Assessment

A. Describing Adverb Phrases
Decide whether each description of an adverb phrase is true (T) or false (F).

_____   1. An adverb phrase can explain how long.

_____   2. An adverb phrase can explain to what extent.

_____   3. An adverb phrase can explain how funny.

_____   4. An adverb phrase can explain how often.

_____   5. An adverb phrase can explain where.

B. Recognizing Adverb Phrases
Decide whether each sentence contains an adverb phrase. Write yes (Y) or no (N).

_____   6. He liked his hair short in the front and longer in the back.

_____   7. The snow has been falling for four hours.

_____   8. He asked for more information.

_____   9. The dog waited.

_____   10. Our flight got in late at night.

C. Identifying Adverb Phrases
Underline the adverb phrase in each sentence.

(11) The new van was purchased by my father. (12) He wanted something big enough for the whole family. (13) A minivan had lots of seats in the back. (14) The van was bright red like an apple (15) and had headlights as bright as the sun. (16) When my dad brought it home, he parked it by the front door. (17) We all peeked out the window. (18) It was as exciting as Christmas! (19) We hadn't had a new car in a long time. (20) Dad told us we could all go for a ride.

Lesson 8-3: Double Negatives Practice

A. Recognizing Double Negatives

Decide whether each word is a negative word and write yes (Y) or no (N).

_____ 1. ever

_____ 2. not

_____ 3. anybody

_____ 4. forever

_____ 5. hardly

B. Identifying Double Negatives

Circle the negative words in each sentence.

6. Giving up won't do you no good.

7. I can't see nothing through my binoculars.

8. We aren't having no one over for Thanksgiving.

9. She didn't do nothing with her talents.

10. I haven't barely seen her all day.

Lesson 8-3: Double Negatives Practice

C. Correcting Double Negatives

Underline the negative words. Then, write each sentence correctly on the lines provided.

(11) Does Bigfoot exist? Many people don't have no clue. (12) Bigfoot hasn't never been spotted. (13) However, lots of people have pretended to be Bigfoot. They haven't never looked that real, though. (14) Scientists say they don't think there's nothing fake about Bigfoot. (15) His tracks don't look like no fake tracks they have seen. (16) In fact, they think there isn't barely any evidence to prove he is fake. (17) Instead, scientists think Bigfoot could be real. They haven't never seen him either, (18) but the facts don't say nothing about him being fake. (19) I know one thing – I don't never want to see Bigfoot! (20) I've never seen nothing like it, and I hope I never will.

11. _____

12. _____

13. _____

14. _____

15. _____

16. _____

17. _____

18. _____

19. _____

20. _____

Lesson 8-3: Double Negatives Assessment

A. Recognizing Double Negatives

Decide whether each word is a negative word and write yes (Y) or no (N).

_____ 1. nobody

_____ 2. anyone

_____ 3. nothing

_____ 4. no

_____ 5. rarely

B. Identifying Double Negatives

Circle the negative words in each sentence.

6. He wasn't rarely available for a meeting.

7. We don't get none of the presents.

8. I don't never get to go anywhere.

9. He can't get no satisfaction.

10. Hasn't nobody heard of this band before?

Lesson 8-3: Double Negatives Assessment

C. Correcting Double Negatives

Underline the negative words. Then, write each sentence correctly on the lines provided.

(11) Nobody has never seen the Loch Ness monster. (12) No one has never caught the Loch Ness monster either. (13) Dr. Robert Kenneth Wilson took a picture of the monster in 1934, but it rarely never appeared after that. (14) Doesn't no one know the monster isn't real? (15) There isn't no evidence to support the monster's existence today. (16) Sailors don't find nothing when they go try to find the monster. (17) Still, they don't never get the hint. (18) Some people say they have seen the monster since 1934, but they can't produce no proof. (19) I think there isn't no monster. (20) Others say I don't know nothing.

11. _____

12. _____

13. _____

14. _____

15. _____

16. _____

17. _____

18. _____

19. _____

20. _____

Name _____   Date _____

Lesson 9-1: Coordinating Conjunctions Practice
Level A

A. Recognizing Coordinating Conjunctions

Determine whether the underlined word is a coordinating conjunction. Write yes (Y) or no (N).

_____ 1. The chicken noodle soup is hot <u>and</u> steamy.

_____ 2. <u>After</u> I woke up, I ate breakfast.

_____ 3. I like tacos and burritos, but <u>not</u> quesadillas.

_____ 4. It was raining, <u>so</u> I wore my raincoat.

_____ 5. We could have fish <u>or</u> steak for dinner.

B. Identifying Coordinating Conjunctions

Select the appropriate coordinating conjunction to complete each sentence.

6. We went to the toy store _____ to the grocery store.
   a. and
   b. nor
   c. or
   d. yet

7. You don't like hamburgers, _____ I made chicken nuggets.
   a. yet
   b. but
   c. so
   d. and

8. We can watch a movie _____ play a game.
   a. but
   b. or
   c. nor
   d. for

9. John likes broccoli, _____ he prefers peas.
   a. but
   b. nor
   c. and
   d. or

10. He can cook fancy meals, _____ he still can't boil water.
   a. nor
   b. yet
   c. for
   d. or

Lesson 9-1: Coordinating Conjunctions Practice
Level A

C. Using Coordinating Conjunctions
Fill in each blank in the paragraph with the appropriate coordinating conjunction.

a. for
b. and
c. nor
d. but

e. or
f. yet
g. so

(11) I don't like Halloween _____ Thanksgiving. (12) My favorite holidays are Christmas _____ Valentine's Day. (13) For Christmas, we either go to my grandma's house _____ my aunt's house. (14) There we exchange presents, _____ we only get one present each. (15) On Valentine's Day, we exchange cards. I always want a card from the person I like, _____ I don't want him to know I like him. (16) I give cards to everyone else, _____ hopefully I will get cards from them, too. (17) My parents give me chocolate _____ flowers. (18) Both holidays are great, _____ I get fun presents. (19) Halloween is scary _____ Thanksgiving is not very exciting, (20) _____ the winter holidays are the best.

Lesson 9-1: Coordinating Conjunctions Practice
Level B

A. Recognizing Coordinating Conjunctions

Write the coordinating conjunction in each sentence. If the sentence does not contain a coordinating conjunction, write **none**.

_____ 1. I won't be in school tomorrow, for I am going on vacation with my family.

_____ 2. Don't you wish it would snow so we could build a snowman?

_____ 3. I like chocolate, but I don't like vanilla.

B. Identifying Coordinating Conjunctions

Match each coordinating conjunction with the sentence it best completes.

a. for   c. nor   e. or   g. so
b. and   d. but   f. yet

_____ 4. You ate all of the chocolate chips, _____ I made peanut butter cookies.

_____ 5. I don't enjoy going to the pool, _____ I do enjoy hiking in the woods.

_____ 6. Getting together with family _____ celebrating birthdays is so much fun.

_____ 7. He had to work late _____ he still made it to the party on time.

_____ 8. She won't go to the movies, _____ will she watch TV.

_____ 9. Have you decided to go to the party _____ are you going to stay home?

_____ 10. He was sure to get scholarships _____ he was a great football player.

Lesson 9-1: Coordinating Conjunctions Practice
Level B

C. Using Coordinating Conjunctions

Complete each sentence with the appropriate coordinating conjunctions.

(11) Christopher Columbus _____ other explorers weren't the first people to come to the United States, (12) _____ were the pilgrims. (13) When Columbus reached the Americas, he thought he was in India, _____ he called the people he saw Indians, (14) _____ they were really Native Americans. (15) In general, the Native Americans were fairly peaceful people _____ they had to share the land and resources with one another. (16) Even when the first settlers came to America, the Native Americans were peaceful people, _____ the settlers still attacked them (17) _____ the Native Americans started to attack back. (18) This led to a lot of bloodshed _____ strife between the Native Americans (19) _____ the settlers. (20) The Native Americans did not have the same powerful weapons as the settlers, _____ they could not put up as big of a fight, which led to many Native Americans dying.

Name _____   Date _____

Lesson 9-1: Coordinating Conjunctions Assessment

A. Recognizing Coordinating Conjunctions

Write the coordinating conjunction in each sentence. If the sentence does not contain a coordinating conjunction, write **none**.

_____   1. I love to eat chocolate chips, but I don't like white chocolate chips.
_____   2. The kittens were running all over the place, so the mother cat pulled them all onto the blanket.
_____   3. Don't you just love autumn with the cool mornings and the leaves changing color on the trees?

B. Identifying Coordinating Conjunctions

Match each coordinating conjunction with the sentence it best completes.

a. for   c. nor   e. or   g. so
b. and   d. but   f. yet

_____ 4. I hadn't been to that theme park in years, _____ it felt I had just been there yesterday.
_____ 5. The family couldn't decide whether to take a trip during the summer _____ have a staycation at home.
_____ 6. He failed his test, _____ his teacher made him stay after school for a tutoring session.
_____ 7. George was sure he would get the job, _____ his best friend worked at the company.
_____ 8. She didn't vacuum the living room, _____ did she load the dishwasher.
_____ 9. I am preparing for a tornado by stocking food in the basement _____ creating an emergency plan.
_____ 10. They were prepared for a zombie invasion, _____ they weren't sure one would ever come.

Lesson 9-1: Coordinating Conjunctions Assessment

C. Using Coordinating Conjunctions

Complete each sentence with the appropriate coordinating conjunctions.

Gravity has always existed, (11) _____ for many years scientists didn't know what it was. The ancient Greeks thought the planets (12) _____ stars just followed a natural path, (13) _____ in the 1500s, scientists discovered that Earth and other planets revolved around the sun. However, they didn't know what caused that to happen, (14) _____ they needed the help of a scientist named Sir Isaac Newton. Newton saw a falling apple (15) _____ thought a force must be acting upon the apple. Apples don't move by themselves (16) _____ do they just start moving from a state of rest. He decided the force was called gravity (17) _____ stated that gravitational forces exist all over. Later, Albert Einstein also studied gravity, (18) _____ he did not agree with all of Newton's ideas. Einstein says gravity comes when space (19) _____ time are warped. (20) Today, scientists are still trying to figure out whether Newton (20) _____ Einstein was correct.

Name _____   Date _____

Lesson 9-2: Correlative Conjunctions Practice
Level A

A. Recognizing Correlative Conjunctions

Determine whether each example is a correlative conjunction. Write yes (Y) or no (N).

_____ 1. either / if

_____ 2. as / as

_____ 3. both / and

_____ 4. these / these

_____ 5. neither / nor

B. Identifying Correlative Conjunctions

Fill in the missing part of each correlative conjunction.

6. _____ / or

7. _____ / as

8. _____ / and

9. whether / _____

10. _____ / but also

C. Using Correlative Conjunctions

Complete the paragraph with the missing correlative conjunctions. If no correlative conjunction is needed, write **none**.

(11) Tomorrow we need to go to the grocery store. We can _____ go to Safegrocer or we can go to Friendly Grocer. (12) _____ Frank Madison or Mercer's will do. (13) As much _____ I would like to go to Mercer's, they don't sell the type of crackers I need. (14) Not only do they not sell the type of crackers I need, _____ they are much more expensive. (15) As for Frank Madison, _____ cheap as they are, they don't carry half of the items on my list. (16) _____ we go to Safegrocer or Friendly Grocer, I know I will find what I need. (17) Safegrocer is not close, _____ it is a little bit cheaper. (18) Friendly Grocer is _____ cheaper, but also it is closer. (19) Either we can drive a little bit more _____ we can save a little bit of money. (20) Whether we go to Safegrocer _____ Friendly Grocer makes no difference to me. You choose.

Name _____   Date _____

Lesson 9-2: Correlative Conjunctions Practice
Level B

A. Recognizing Correlative Conjunctions
Circle the correlative conjunctions.

my / and	these / those	not only / but also
either / or	these / and	if ever / for always
neither / nor	both / and	whether / or

B. Identifying Correlative Conjunctions
Use the following words to put together five pairs of correlating conjunctions. Note: Some words may be used more than once.

either   whether   neither   both   not   or   nor   and   but

6. _____ / _____
7. _____ / _____
8. _____ / _____
9. _____ / _____
10. _____ / _____

C. Using Correlative Conjunctions
Complete the paragraph with the missing correlative conjunctions. If no correlative conjunction is needed, write **none**.

(11) Not only is Valentine's Day my least favorite holiday, _____ it is the saddest holiday. (12) Whether you have a boyfriend _____ don't have anyone to celebrate with, the holiday sucks. (13) If you have a boyfriend, _____ he'll forget to get you something or he'll get you something you don't like. (14) And if you don't have a boyfriend he'll _____ forget to get you something nor get you something you don't like. (15) _____ scenarios are no fun and make Valentine's Day my least favorite holiday. (16) Wait! What's this in my locker? A valentine? _____ have I never gotten a valentine before, but also this one is really cute. (17) I wonder _____ it's from, Joey or Christopher. (18) Whether it's from Joey _____ Christopher, I'll be really excited. (19) Oh, it's from Lenny. Lenny is not who I hoped it was from _____ I guess it's better than nothing. (20) I'm still _____ a fan of Valentine's Day, but I'm happy I got a valentine this year.

Name _____   Date _____

Lesson 9-2: Correlative Conjunctions Assessment

A. Recognizing Correlative Conjunctions

Determine whether each example is a correlative conjunction pair. Write yes (Y) or no (N).

_____ 1. each / for

_____ 2. mine / my

_____ 3. both / and

_____ 4. not only / but also

_____ 5. neither / nor

B. Identifying Correlative Conjunctions

Fill in the missing part of each correlative conjunction. No correlative conjunction repeats.

6. whether / _____   9. either / _____

7. _____ / nor   10. _____ / but

8. _____ / and

C. Using Correlative Conjunctions

Complete the paragraph with the missing correlative conjunctions. If no correlative conjunction is needed, write **none**.

(11) Not only does Erica wear stylish clothes _____ she gets great deals on them.

(12) _____ she buys them at Clothes 4 Less or she goes to local thrift stores.

(13) Whether you like _____ hate to shop at thrift stores, you have to admit you can get some good deals there. (14) _____ the outlet mall nor the clearance racks at department stores have as good of deals as thrift stores. (15) _____ can you get good deals, but also you can find a lot of unique pieces. (16) For example, Erica's favorite shirt is a vintage rock band t-shirt that she bought not at a rock concert _____ at a thrift store. (17) Either someone got tired of the band _____ dropped the shirt off by accident. (18) _____ the thrift store got the shirt on purpose or by accident, it still turned out to be an awesome deal for Erica. (19) To get the best deals, however, Erica has to go shopping every week. She _____ goes shopping on Monday or Tuesday. (20) They put out new inventory on _____ Monday and Tuesday.

Name _____   Date _____

Lesson 9-3: Interjections Practice

A. Understanding Interjections

Decide whether each statement used to describe interjections is true (T) or false (F).

_____ 1. Interjections are used to show weak emotions.

_____ 2. Interjections may exclaim, protest, or demand.

_____ 3. Interjections never use an exclamation point.

_____ 4. Interjections are frequently used in formal writing.

_____ 5. Interjections are sometimes set apart by commas.

B. Identifying Interjections

Choose the appropriate interjection for each sentence.

6. _____! Please tell me this isn't happening!
   a. Yuck
   b. Aww
   c. Hurray
   d. No

7. _____! I will marry you!
   a. Yummy
   b. Yes
   c. Ouch
   d. Yuck

8. _____! You're a great chef.
   a. Yum
   b. Oh, no
   c. Yuck
   d. Ouch

9. _____! I'm so glad you got the new job.
   a. Hurray
   b. A-ha
   c. Oh, no
   d. No

10. _____! I can't believe this is happening again.
   a. Oh, no
   b. No
   c. Grr
   d. Yes

 ©2015 Erin Cobb • CD-105007

Lesson 9-3: Interjections Practice

C. Identifying Interjections in Writing

Underline the interjection in each sentence. Then, write whether it expresses a **positive** or **negative** emotion.

(11) Goodness! The baby just let out a large burp. (12) Oh no! I forgot the burp cloth. It got on my shirt. (13) Man! This is my favorite shirt too. (14) Argh! I officially hate babysitting. (15) Awww! Now the baby is cooing. (16) "Hey, you're kind of cute little guy, even if you just spit up on my favorite shirt. (17) Your parents pay me good money to babysit, too." Oh yeah! (18) I can't wait to get paid for this job. Sweet! (19) I'm going to have enough money to buy that shirt I've always wanted. Yes! (20) Man, I have been wanting that shirt forever.

11. _____

12. _____

13. _____

14. _____

15. _____

16. _____

17. _____

18. _____

19. _____

20. _____

Lesson 9-3: Interjections Assessment

A. Understanding Interjections

Decide whether each statement used to describe interjections is true (T) or false (F).

_____   1. Interjections exclaim something.

_____   2. Interjections protest something.

_____   3. Interjections sometimes show no emotion.

_____   4. Interjections demand something.

_____   5. Interjections always end with an exclamation point.

B. Identifying Interjections

Circle the interjection in each sentence.

6. Ew! Don't go in the bathroom!

7. Whew, I'm so glad it's over.

8. You're taking us to the amusement park? Yippee!

9. There are two spiders over there. Eek!

10. No way!

Lesson 9-3: Interjections Assessment

C. Identifying Interjections in Writing

Underline each interjection and write whether it expresses a **positive** or **negative** emotion.

(11) "I don't want to be your best friend anymore," Lisa said. "Ouch, that hurts," I said, (12) "Look, I'm sorry. Argh! I wish I hadn't been so stupid." (13) "Duh! Sure you're sorry now," Lisa retorted. (14) "Yes! I was sorry when it happened too, I just wasn't thinking," I said. (15) "Well, you never seem to do much thinking," she said. (16) "Ouch, that stings," I replied. (17) "Great! You deserve it," she said. (18) "Hey, I know I made a mistake, but you don't have to be so mean," I replied. (19) "Ooh, I'm being mean?" Lisa said. (20) "Oops! I just wasn't thinking."

11. _____

12. _____

13. _____

14. _____

15. _____

16. _____

17. _____

18. _____

19. _____

20. _____

Answer Key

Page 4
Lesson 0.5 Practice
1. g; 2. c; 3. h; 4. e; 5. d; 6. a; 7. f; 8. b; 9. Johannah–noun, really–adverb, likes–verb, apples–noun, and–conjunction, cherries-noun; 10. December – noun, is–verb, my– pronoun, favorite–adjective, month–noun; 11. pronoun; 12. adjective; 13. verb; 14. noun; 15. interjection; 16. adjective 17. preposition; 18. pronoun; 19. noun; 20. conjunction

Page 5
Lesson 0.5 Assessment
1. T; 2. T; 3. F; 4. T; 5. T; 6. Stacy–noun, beautiful–adjective, doll-noun, needs-verb, clothes-noun; 7. She -pronoun, is-verb, hungry-adjective, so-conjunction, she-pronoun, will eat-verb; 8. noun; 9. pronoun; 10. interjection; 11. adverb; 12. verb; 13. adjective; 14. verb; 15. pronoun; 16. conjunction; 17. adjective; 18. adverb; 19. verb; 20. adjective

Pages 6–7
Lesson 1-1 Practice
(For #1-5, students should only use "c" if no other rule applies.) 1. a, b; 2. c; 3. a, d, f; 4. e, a; 5. b, a; 6. N; 7. N; 8. N; 9. Y; 10. Y; 11. France; 12. Mrs. Lovelace; 13. International Tours; 14. Paris, France; 15. Longchamp Palace; 16. Cannes; 17. NE; 18. I; 19. French; 20. French for Tourists

Pages 8–9
Lesson 1-1 Assessment
(For #1-5, students should only use "c" if no other rule applies.) 1. a, f; 2. f, d; 3. b; 4. d, a; 5. a; 6. Y; 7. N; 8. Y; 9. N; 10. Y; 11. years; 12. NE; 13. May; 14. Uncle, Aunt; 15. Jersey; 16. Mary's Hospital; 17. Sun; 18. Harriet Stormer; 19. uncle; 20. Mrs.

Pages 10–11
Lesson 1-2 Practice
1. e, f; 2. h, d; 3. g; 4. a, h, g; 5. a, h, d; 6. Y; 7. N; 8. N; 9. Y; 10. Y; 11. , you, up,; 12. mean,; 13. , nodded his head; 14. Well,; 15. NC; 16. July 12,; 17. Well,; 18. then,; 19. , but; 20. something,

Pages 12–13
Lesson 1-2 Assessment
1. d, a; 2. g; 3. g, a; 4. e, f; 5. a; 6. Y; 7. N; 8. Y; 9. Y; 10. N; 11. summer, says,;12. , but; 13. summer, Fargo,; 14. Oklahoma, New York,; 15. going,; 16. NC; 17. Alaska, Territories,; 18. adventure,; 19. NC; 20. , but

Page 14
Lesson 1-3 Practice
1. P; 2. C; 3. C; 4. P; 5. C; 6. IC; 7. C; 8. IC; 9. C; 10. IC; 11. NA; 12. isn't; 13. It's; 14. NA; 15. Canadians'; 16. NA; 17. NA; 18. aren't; 19. NA; 20. NA

Page 15
Lesson 1-3 Assessment
1. C; 2. P; 3. C; 4. C; 5. P; 6. C; 7. IC; 8. C; 9. IC; 10. IC; 11. Shakespeare's; 12. Laertes's; 13. Odysseus's; 14. son's; 15. Polonius's; 16. doesn't; 17. NA; 18. sister's; 19. NA; 20. that's

Pages 16–17
Lesson 1-4 Practice
1. a, b; 2. d; 3. e; 4. f; 5. Y; 6. Y; 7. N; 8. Y; 9. Y; 10. "Dogs and Their Bones"; 11. None; 12. "Dogs are very possessive,"; 13. None; 14. "Why do you bury your bones?"; 15. "Arf!"; 16. "What does that mean?"; 17. "It means that I bury my bones because they taste better that way!"; 18. None; 19. "Ms. Keeler, my dog says he buries his bones because they taste better that way, not to keep them away from other dogs."; 20. None

Pages 18–19
Lesson 1-4 Assessment
1. a; 2. e, f; 3. d; 4. b; 5. c; 6. Y; 7. N; 8. N; 9. Y; 10. Y; 11. "Tomorrow, we are going to have a big test,"; 12. "so you'd better study hard tonight."; 13. "Why do we have to take another test?"; 14. "Yeah," Lisa piped up, "why can't we write a paper or something?"; 15. None; 16. "Tonight, said Mrs. Carter, "instead of studying for your test, I want you to write a poem about your favorite song."; 17. "Row, Row, Row Your Boat"; 18. "The Farmer in the Dell."; 19. "What are you going to write about, Lisa?"; 20. None

Answer Key

Pages 20–21
Lesson 1-5 Practice
1. a; 2. f; 3. c; 4. e, d; 5. d; 6. Y; 7. N; 8. Y; 9. Y; 10. N;
11. three; 12. five; 13. eight; 14. Eight; 15. 25; 16. 50;
17. 35; 18. two; 19. ten; 20. 1,000

Pages 22–23
Lesson 1-5 Assessment
1. d; 2. c; 3. a; 4. a, f; 5. e; 6. Y; 7. N; 8. N; 9. Y; 10. Y;
11. Six; 12. 2; 13. 4; 14. 13; 15. 18; 16. 38; 17. 40; 18. six;
19. 2013; 20. seven

Page 24
Lesson 1-6 Practice
1. a; 2. e; 3. a; 4. d; 5. b; 6. c; 7. d; 8. b; 9. d; 10. c;
11. kids; 12. superheroes; 13. children; 14. fans;
15. letters; 16. heroes; 17. wishes; 18. men;
19. costumes; 20. lives

Page 25
Lesson 1-6 Assessment
1. a; 2. b; 3. a; 4. d; 5. b; 6. c; 7. d; 8. d; 9. b; 10. b;
11. phases; 12. countries; 13. places; 14. societies;
15. days; 16. eclipses; 17. features; 18. craters;
19. quarters; 20. centuries

Page 26
Lesson 1-7 Practice
1. c; 2. d; 3. a; 4. b; 5. e; 6. N; 7. Y; 8. N; 9. Y; 10. N;
11. conscious; 12. farther; 13. breath; 14. since; 15. too;
16. two; 17. than; 18. effect; 19. too; 20. conscious

Page 27
Lesson 1-7 Assessment
1. a; 2. c; 3. d; 4. b; 5. e; 6. N; 7. Y; 8. Y; 9. N; 10. Y;
11. altar; 12. there; 13. aloud; 14. aisle; 15. isle;
16. there; 17. sight; 18. breathe; 19. lose; 20. isle

Page 28
Lesson 2-1 Practice
1. d; 2. c; 3. b; 4. a; 5. d and a; 6. b; 7. a; 8. c; 9. b;
10. c; 11. ?, interrogative; 12. ., declarative; 13. !,
exclamatory; 14. ., declarative; 15. ?, interrogative;
16. ., declarative; 17. !, exclamatory; 18. ., declarative;
19. ? interrogative; 20. ., imperative

Page 29
Lesson 2-1 Assessment
1. b; 2. a; 3. d; 4. c; 5. a; 6. d; 7. a; 8. c; 9. b; 10. d; 11. ?,
interrogative; 12. ?, interrogative; 13. ., declarative;
14. !, exclamatory; 15. !, exclamatory; 16. ., declarative;
17. ?, interrogative; 18. ., imperative; 19. !, exclamatory;
20. ., imperative

Pages 30–31
Lesson 2-2 Practice Level A
1. b; 2. a; 3. d; 4. c; 5. b; 6. a; 7. b; 8. a; 9. b; 10. b;
11. Persians; 12. The Persians; 13. was; 14. had a
democracy; 15. They; 16. decided; 17. They; 18. beat
the Persians; 19. They; 20. worked

Pages 32–33
Lesson 2-2 Practice Level B
1. a; 2. d; 3. b; 4. c; 5. a; 6. b; 7. a; 8. b; 9. a; 10. d;
11. moved to the United States from Mexico; 12. was;
13. He; 14. Most of the kids; 15. was; 16. Jacob; 17. The
mean Jacob; 18. would make fun of the way that Carlos
talked; 19. bothered Carlos so much; 20. Carlos

Pages 34–35
Lesson 2-2 Assessment
1. b; 2. a; 3. d; 4. c; 5. a; 6. a; 7. b; 8. a; 9. b; 10. c;
11. food; 12. became; 13. they; 14. would bury it in the
ground; 15. would dig up their bones; 16. This game;
17. dogs' instincts; 18. They; 19. was just like their
ancestors did; 20. Some dogs, they

Answer Key

Pages 36–37
Lesson 2-3 Practice Level A
1. S; 2. P; 3. S; 4. N; 5. P; 6. b; 7. c; 8. a; 9. d; 10. e;
11. S + P;12. S + P + P; 13. S + P + P; 14. S + S + P + P;
15. S + P; 16. S + S + P; 17. S + S + P; 18. S + P + P;
19. S + P; 20. S + P

Pages 38–39
Lesson 2-3 Practice Level B
1. S; 2. P; 3. N; 4. S; 5. P; 6. d; 7. b; 8. e; 9. a; 10. c;
11. S + P; 12. S + P + P; 13. S + S + S + P; 14. S + P + P;
15. S + S + S + P + P; 16. S + P + P + P; 17. S + P + P;
18. S + S + P + P; 19. S + P; 20. S + P

Pages 40–41
Lesson 2-3 Assessment
1. S; 2. P; 3. N; 4. S; 5. P; 6. d; 7. b; 8. a; 9. c; 10. e;
11. S + S + P; 12. S + P + P; 13. S + S + S + P; 14. S + P + P;
15. S + P + P; 16. S + S + P + P; 17. S + S + P + P + P;
18. S + P + S + P; 19. S + S + P; 20. S + P

Page 42
Lesson 2-4 Practice Level A
1. S; 2. C; 3. S; 4. S; 5. C; 6. , so; 7. , but; 8. , so; 9. , or;
10. , and; 11. , but; 12. , but; 13. ; OR, but; 14. , so;
15. , and; 16. , but; 17. , so OR, and; 18. , and; 19. , so;
20. , or

Page 43
Lesson 2-4 Practice Level B
1. S; 2. C; 3. S; 4. C; 5. C; 6. , so; 7. , and; 8. , but;
9. , and; 10. ;; 11. , and; 12. , and; 13. ;; 14. , and;
15. and; 16. , because; 17. None; 18. , but; 19. , and;
20. , so

Page 44
Lesson 2-4 Assessment
1. C; 2. S; 3. S; 4. C; 5. S; 6. , so; 7. , but; 8. , but; 9. , and;
10. , and; 11. and; 12. and; 13. , but; 14. , so; 15. , and
OR , yet; 16. , and OR ;; 17. , and; 18. ;; 19. , and;
20. , and OR ;

Page 45
Lesson 2-5 Practice Level A
1. D; 2. I; 3. D; 4. D; 5. I; 6. d; 7. b; 8. c; 9. e; 10. a;
11. Once I get home . . .(Once); 12. because it needs .
. . (because); 13. After I do my . . . (After); 14. even if
Judge Christopher . . . (even if); 15. though sometimes
my mom . . . (though); 16. Rather than . . . (Rather);
17. unless she has . . . (unless); 18. as long as she does
them . . . (as long as); 19. whereas I think that's . . .
(whereas); 20. Until she stops . . . (Until)

Page 46
Lesson 2-5 Practice Level B
1. D; 2. D; 3. D; 4. I; 5. I; 6. e; 7. a; 8. d; 9. c; 10. b;
11. When Erica went off to college (when); 12. since
the day she was born (since); 13. even though it wasn't
cool to take a stuffed animal to school (even though);
14. even with Mr. Cuddles (even with); 15. even though
others could see him (even though); 16. whenever
kids came to her room (whenever); 17. because he
was special (because); 18. after going to class one day
(after); 19. if she didn't have Mr. Cuddles (if); 20. until
she found Mr. Cuddles under the bed (until)

Page 47
Lesson 2-5 Assessment
1. D; 2. I; 3. D; 4. D; 5. I; 6. a; 7. d; 8. c; 9. e; 10. b;
11. As long as people could remember (as/as); 12. even
though the townspeople tried (even though);
13. until they were full (until); 14. since nothing worked
(since); 15. although they tried everything (although);
16. until a piper came to town (until);
17. Whether he knew what he was doing or not
(Whether); 18. Whenever he played his pipe
(Whenever); 19. until he stopped (until); 20. until one
day they followed him right out of town (until)

Page 48
Lesson 2-6 Practice
1. a; 2. c; 3. b; 4. F; 5. S; 6. RO; 7. RO; 8. S; 9. RO; 10. F;
11. F; 12. S; 13. RO; 14. F; 15. S; 16. S; 17. S; 18. RO;
19. S; 20. S

Answer Key

Page 49
Lesson 2-6 Assessment
1. c; 2. b; 3. c; 4. a; 5. a; 6. S; 7. F; 8. S; 9. RO; 10. F; 11. F;
12. S; 13. RO; 14. S; 15. F; 16. S; 17. S; 18. RO; 19. S; 20. S

Page 50
Lesson 3-1 Practice
1. P; 2. P; 3. C; 4. P; 5. C; 6. C; 7. P; 8. P; 9. C; 10. C;
11. Temple, Ancient Greece–P; 12. artists, time–C;
13. sculptures, statue–C, Jupiter–P; 14. ivory, jewels–C;
15. gardens–C; Temple–P, statues–C; 16. athlete,
games–C; 17. sculptor, statue–C; 18. statues, gardens–C;
Temple–P; 19. Athletics, talents–C, Olympics–P;
20. musicians, poets–C

Page 51
Lesson 3-1 Assessment
1. P; 2. C; 3. C; 4. P; 5. C; 6. C; 7. P; 8. C; 9. P; 10. P;
11. god–C, Hercules–P, strength–C; 12. prowess–C;
13. people, temple–C, Olympia–P; 14. Hercules–P,
events–C; 15. throwing, wrestling, boxing, races–C;
16. Hercules–P, umpire, games, crown, leaves, winner–C;
17. games, group, people–C; 18. Spartans–P;
19. athletes–C; 20. majority–C, Olympics–P, awards–C

Page 52
Lesson 3-2 Practice
1. C; 2. A; 3. C; 4. A; 5. C; 6. C; 7. A; 8. A; 9. A; 10. C;
Note: Explanations will vary. 11. clouds–C; 12. Clouds–C,
calmness–A; 13. sky–C; 14. shapes, clouds–C; 15.
knights, ogres–C; 16. soldiers–C; peace–A; 17. heroes–C;
strength–A; 18. clouds–C, imagination–A; 19. ideas––A,
stories–C; 20. clouds–C, inspirations–A

Page 53
Lesson 3-2 Assessment
1. C; 2. A; 3. C; 4. A; 5. A; 6. A; 7. C; 8. C; 9. C; 10. A;
Note: Explanations will vary. 11. girl–C, imagination–A;
12. stories–C, mind–A; 13. beauty, adventure–A;
14. dragons, fairies–C; 15. mushrooms, flowers–C;
16. jigs, mountains–C; 17. energy, creativity–A;
18. animals, princesses–C; 19. forests, castles–C;
20. dreams–A

Page 54
Lesson 3-3 Practice
1. e; 2. d; 3. b; 4. c; 5. d; 6. d; 7. a; 8. b; 9. c; 10. a;
11. witches; 12. goblins; 13. streets; 14. bags;
15. candies; 16. treats; 17. wolves; 18. treasures;
19. festivities; 20. beds

Page 55
Lesson 3-3 Assessment
1. a; 2. b; 3. a; 4. c; 5. d; 6. b; 7. a; 8. a; 9. b; 10. c;
11. men; 12. mice; 13. soldiers; 14. boys; 15. warriors;
16. fighters; 17. recruits; 18. lives; 19. countries;
20. identities

Page 56
Lesson 3-4 Practice
1. b; 2. a; 3. d; 4. c; 5. a; 6. c; 7. a; 8. b; 9. b; 10. b;
11. Sarah's, Jackie's, and Alex's; 12. people's; 13. Sarah's;
14. Jackie's; 15. Alex's; 16. girls'; 17. mom and dad's;
18. neighborhood's; 19. crosswalks'; 20. friend's

Page 57
Lesson 3-4 Assessment
1. a; 2. b; 3. a; 4. c; 5. a; 6. a; 7. c; 8. b; 9. b; 10. c;
11. Egyptians'; 12. god's; 13. A's; 14. L's;
15. archaeologists'; 16. pyramids'; 17. kings';
18. royalty's; 19. people's; 20. Egyptians'

Page 58
Lesson 4-1 Practice Level A
1. A; 2. L; 3. H; 4. A; 5. L, H; 6. H; 7. A; 8. L; 9. L, H; 10. A;
11. am running–H; 12. is–L; 13. will run–H; 14. was–L;
15. am–L; 16. looked–A; 17. is–L; 18. hope–L; 19. will–H;
20. feel–L

Page 59
Lesson 4-1 Practice Level B
1. A; 2. L; 3. H; 4. A; 5. H; 6. A; 7. L; 8. A; 9. A; 10. L;
11. must–H; 12. are–L; 13. eat–A; 14. can–H; 15.
opens–A; 16. gets–A; 17. will–H; 18. feel–L; 19. am–L;
20. can hear–A

Answer Key

Page 60

Lesson 4-1 Assessment

1. A; 2. H; 3. L; 4. A; 5. L; 6. H; 7. A; 8. A; 9. H; 10. L or H;
11. am–H; 12. study–A; 13. complete–A; 14. get–A;
15. am–H; 16. am–L; 17. takes–A; 18. feel–L;
19. seems–L; 20. will–H

Pages 61–62

Lesson 4-2 Practice Level A

1. PN; 2. PA; 3. PA; 4. PA; 5. PA; 6. mean, PA; 7. doctor,
PN; 8. mad, PA; 9. plump, PA; 10. suspect, PN; 11. John,
was, kid; 12. He, was, worker; 13. He, was, determined;
14. John, became, astronaut; 15. He, is, astronaut;
16. John, has been, hero; 17. He, is, guy; 18. NLV;
19. NLV; 20. NLV

Pages 63–64

Lesson 4-2 Practice Level B

1. PN; 2. PN; 3. NE; 4. PA; 5. PA; 6. Friends/are/people
(noun); 7. Dogs/seem/ happy (adjective); 8. Scarlet/
does not seem/scared (adjective); 9. nose/becomes/red
(adjective); 10. irises/smell/beautiful (adjective);
11. book, PN; 12. author, PN; 13. monster, PN;
14. zombie, PN; 15. murderer, PN;16. bad, PA;
17. angry, PA; 18. lonely, PA; 19. compassionate, PA;
20. murderer, PN

Pages 65–66

Lesson 4-2 Assessment

1. PA; 2. PA; 3. PN; 4. NE; 5. PN; 6. father/became/
man (noun); 7. face/became/concerned (adjective);
8. footsteps/grew/louder (adjective); 9. I/feel/person
(noun);10. sisters/are/people (noun); 11. element, PN;
12. element, PN; 13. 1868, PN; 14. odd, PA;
15. ball, PN; 16. responsible, PA; 17. sun god, PN;
18. form, PN; 19. gas, PN; 20. simple, PA

Pages 67–68

Lesson 4-3 Practice

1. c; 2. f; 3. d; 4. a; 5. e; 6. b; 7. a; 8. b; 9. d; 10. c;
11. present; 12. future perfect; 13. present perfect;
14. present; 15. future; 16. present; 17. past; 18. past;
19. present perfect; 20. present

Pages 69–70

Lesson 4-3 Assessment

1. a; 2. d; 3. c; 4. e; 5. f; 6. b; 7. d; 8. b; 9. d; 10. c;
11. present; 12. present perfect; 13. present; 14. past;
15. past; 16. present; 17. future; 18. present; 19. future
perfect; 20. future

Page 71

Lesson 4-4 Practice Level A

1. b; 2. a; 3. c; 4. d; 5. b; 6. c; 7. a; 8. d; 9. infinitive;
10. past participle; 11. infinitive; 12. present participle;
13. past; 14. past participle; 15. past; 16. past;
17. present participle; 18. infinitive; 19. infinitive;
20. infinitive

Page 72

Lesson 4-4 Practice Level B

1. d; 2. c; 3. b; 4. a; 5. b; 6. c; 7. a; 8. d; 9. are going;
10. have gone; 11. went; 12. to visit; 13. are visiting;
14. is feeling; 15. are living; 16. are driving; 17. am
wishing; 18. moved; 19. had; 20. have lived

Page 73

Lesson 4-4 Assessment

1. b; 2. a; 3. c; 4. d; 5. d; 6. b; 7. c; 8. a; 9. came;
10. to pay; 11. is paying; 12. paid; 13. has paid; 14. pay;
15. ordered, drank; 16. have drunk; 17. are drinking;
18. are eating; 19. are meeting; 20. have met

Page 74

Lesson 4-5 Practice Level A

1. DO: 2. IO; 3. IO; 4. DO; 5. IO; 6. IO; 7. DO; 8. IO; 9. N;
10. N; 11. DO–postcard, IO–mom; 12. DO–postcard,
IO–me; 13. DO–picture; 14. DO–picture;
15. DO–snowman, IO–me: 16. DO–sandcastle, IO–mom;
17. DO–something, IO–each other; 18. DO–shovel,
IO–me; 19. DO–scarf, IO–her; 20. DO–correspondence

Answer Key

©2015 Erin Cobb • CD-105007

Page 75

Lesson 4-5 Practice Level B

1. DO; 2. IO; 3. IO; 4. DO; 5. N; 6. DO; 7. IO; 8. DO;
9. IO; 10. N; 11. DO–surprise, IO–us; 12. DO–break,
IO–teachers; 13. DO–teachers, IO–spa; 14. DO–party;
15. DO–gym; 16. DO–requests, IO–students;
17. DO–students, IO–snacks; 18. DO–games;
19. DO–teachers; 20. DO–thanks, IO–principal

Page 76

Lesson 4-5 Assessment

1. DO; 2. IO; 3. IO; 4. DO; 5. IO; 6. IO; 7. DO; 8. IO; 9. IO;
10. N; 11. DO–bill, IO–us; 12. DO–wallet; 13. DO–wallet,
IO–him; 14. DO–credit card; 15. DO–bill and card,
IO–waiter; 16. DO–restaurant; 17. DO–keys, IO–me;
18. DO–car, IO–house; 19. DO–ticket; 20. DO–ticket,
IO–dad

Page 77

Lesson 5-1 Practice Level A

1. b; 2. b; 3. a; 4. b; 5. a; 6. at; 7. toward; 8. between;
9. at; 10. by; 11. outside–where; 12. above–where;
13. Despite–how; 14. in–where; 15. behind–where;
16. underneath–where; 17. beyond–where; 18. on–
where; 19. beneath–where; 20. across–where

Page 78

Lesson 5-1 Practice Level B

1. a; 2. a; 3. b; 4. d; 5. c; 6. in; 7. at; 8. among; 9. since;
10. without; 11. on–where; 12. with–how; 13. until–
when; 14. from–where; 15. in–where/how; 16. into–
how; 17. inside–where;18. out–how; 19. from–where/
how; 20. through–where

Page 79

Lesson 5-1 Assessment

1. a, b; 2. d; 3. b; 4. c; 5. a; 6. from; 7. of; 8. along;
9. on; 10. inside; 11. in–where; 12. across–where/how;
13. inside–where; 14. on–where; 15. up–where/how;
16. through–where/how; 17. before–when; 18. while–
when;19. about–where/how; 20. in–where

Page 80

Lesson 5-2 Practice Level A

1. P; 2. PP; 3. O; 4. above the clouds; 5. below the radar;
6. of the night; 7. to the mall, in the morning; 8. after
the holiday; 9. beneath the mistletoe; 10. against the
wall; 11. on our porch, porch; 12. on the first column,
column; 13. around the second column, column;
14. over the porch light, light; 15. beneath the porch
light, light;16. below the porch, porch; 17. above the
front door, door; 18. under the mistletoe, mistletoe;
19. through the door, door; 20. without the
decorations, decorations

Page 81

Lesson 5-2 Practice Level B

1. PP; 2. O; 3. P; 4. at the bakery; 5. around the house;
6. past the bank; 7. through the woods; 8. over the
river; 9. since 1993; 10. down the hill; 11. deep in the
woods, woods; 12. along the river, river; 13. between
the trees, trees; 14. across the river, river; 15. by the old
oak tree, tree; 16. under the bushes, bushes; 17. inside
the last bush, bush; 18. under that bush, bush; 19. in
that place, place; 20. with my thoughts, thoughts

Page 82

Lesson 5-2 Assessment

1. P; 2. PP; 3. O; 4. across town; 5. in my backpack;
6. after the game; 7. along the beach; 8. from school;
9. under my fleece blanket; 10. down the street;
11. to my grandpa's beach house, house; in North
Carolina, North Carolina; 12. during the summer,
summer; 13. in the spring, spring; 14. down to North
Carolina, North Carolina; 15. on the beach, beach;
16. in the sand, sand; 17. in the water, water; 18. on
the water, water; 19. across the dunes, dunes; 20. to my
grandpa's beach house, house

Answer Key

Page 83
Lesson 5-3 Practice Level A
1. ADV; 2. ADJ; 3. ADV; 4. ADJ; 5. ADJ; 6. of milk; 7. with his tools; 8. Tomorrow morning; 9. Every Monday; 10. with the toys; 11. down the street, verb; 12. with white feet, noun; 13. in the bushes, verb; 14. in my arms, verb; 15. with the rabbit, verb; 16. for his dinner, noun; 17. for the rabbit, noun; 18. Tomorrow morning, verb; 19. in the house, verb; 20. all day long, verb

Page 84
Lesson 5-3 Practice Level B
1. ADJ; 2. ADV; 3. ADJ; 4. ADV; 5. ADV; 6. of candy; 7. at the airport; 8. without care; 9. with great speed; 10. on the ground; 11. with a big heart–noun; 12. of great wisdom–noun; 13. without learning something new–verb; 14. from Harvard University–verb; 15. from life experience–verb; 16. to my grandma's house–verb; 17. late at night–verb; 18. in the early morning–adj; 19. with my problems–verb; 20. with lots of love–adj

Page 85
Lesson 5-3 Assessment
1. ADJ; 2. ADV; 3. ADJ; 4. ADV; 5. ADV; 6. of pickles; 7. on the train; 8. late at night; 9. every morning; 10. with his father; 11. of old coins–noun; 12. by my father–verb; 13. by his father–verb; 14. on the shelf–noun; 15. above my bed–verb; 16. in the morning–verb; 17. in the box–noun; 18. from everywhere in the world–noun; 19. during the war–verb; 20. at night–verb

Page 86
Lesson 6-1 Practice Level A
1. e; 2. c; 3. b; 4. a; 5. f; 6. d; 7. those, you; 8. Our; 9. you, yourself; 10. whose, that; 11. you, you–personal; those–demonstrative; 12. I–personal, them–personal; 13. It–personal; 14. they–personal; 15. You–personal; 16. me–personal; 17. You–personal; 18. yourself–reflexive; 19. I'm–personal, yours–possessive; 20. mine–possessive; NOTE: In 19-20, accept student answers that name *I* (I'm) and *they* (they'll) as pronouns.

Page 87
Lesson 6-1 Practice Level B
1. e; 2. b; 3. c; 4. f; 5. d; 6. a; 7. anyone; 8. This; 9. She, herself; 10. He, those, somebody; 11. you–personal; 12. who–interrogative; 13. I–personal; 14. it–personal; 5. myself–reflexive; 16. you–personal; 17. I–personal; 18. you–personal; 19. this–demonstrative; 20. something–indefinite

Page 88
Lesson 6-1 Assessment
1. e; 2. c; 3. b; 4. a; 5. a; 6. f; 7. whom, I; 8. me; 9. I, it, myself; 10. What, you; 11. This–demonstrative; 12. I–personal; 13. I–personal; 14. myself–reflexive; 15. my–possessive, me–personal; 16. we–personal; 17. my–possessive; 18. me–personal; 19. He–personal; 20. several–indefinite

Page 89
Lesson 6-2 Practice Level A
1. d; 2. e; 3. c; 4. a; 5. b; 6. a; 7. a; 8. e; 9. d; 10. f; 11. These; 12. his; 13. it, him; 14. them; 15. they; 16. my; 17. myself; 18. him; 19. my; 20. themselves

Page 90
Lesson 6-2 Practice Level B
1. a; 2. c; 3. e; 4. d; 5. b; 6. d; 7. c; 8. a; 9. c; 10. a; 11. what; 12. my; 13. I; 14. her; 15. it; 16. anything; 17. something; 18. someone; 19. who; 20. something

Page 91
Lesson 6-2 Assessment
1. d; 2. b; 3. e; 4. a; 5. c; 6. b; 7. e; 8. d; 9. f; 10. a; 11. my; 12. We; 13. her; 14. she; 15. We; 16. everything; 17. I; 18. ourselves; 19. No one; 20. our

Page 92
Lesson 7-1 Practice Level A
1. d; 2. c; 3. a; 4. b; 5. d; 6. a; 7. a; 8. c; 9. a; 10. b; 11. proper; 12. proper; 13. demonstrative; 14. proper; 15. proper; 16. describer; 17. describer; 18. demonstrative; 19. article; 20. describer

Answer Key

Page 93
Lesson 7-1 Practice Level B
1. d; 2. c; 3. a; 4. b; 5. b; 6. d; 7. a; 8. c; 9. a; 10. b;
11. demonstrative; 12. article; 13. proper; 14. describer;
15. proper; 16. proper; 17. demonstrative; 18. proper;
19. describer; 20. describer

Page 94
Lesson 7-1 Assessment
1. b; 2. a; 3. d; 4. c; 5. c; 6. d; 7. b; 8. a; 9. a; 10. a;
11. demonstrative; 12. describer; 13. article;
14. describer; 15. demonstrative; 16. describer,
describer; 17. demonstrative; 18. demonstrative;
19. describer; 20. article

Page 95
Lesson 7-2 Practice
1. c; 2. a; 3. b; 4. C; 5. S; 6. C; 7. S; 8. C; 9. S; 10. S;
11. worst; 12. later; 13. colder; 14. nastiest; 15. earlier;
16. coldest; 17. best; 18. better; 19. loneliest; 20. worse

Page 96
Lesson 7-2 Assessment
1. b; 2. c; 3. a; 4. S; 5. C; 6. S; 7. P; 8. C; 9. S; 10. S;
11. best; 12. clearer; 13. loudest; 14. louder; 15. most
beautiful; 16. more beautiful; 17. nicest; 18. best;
19. better; 20. most awesome

Page 97
Lesson 8-1 Practice Level A
1. c; 2. b; 3. a; 4. e; 5. b; 6. here; 7. quickly;
8. occasionally; 9. below; 10. next week; 11. truthfully–
how; 12. honestly–how; 13. really–to what extent;
14. very–to what extent; 15. simply–how; 16.
amazingly–how; 17. still–how long; 18. completely–
how; 19. absolutely–to what extent; 20. really–to what
extent

Page 98
Lesson 8-1 Practice Level B
1. b; 2. a; 3. a; 4. b; 5. e; 6. enthusiastically;
7. precariously; 8. seldom, really; 9. utterly, very;
10. upstairs; 11. never–time; 12. late–time; 13. usually–
degree; 14. too–degree; 15. always–degree; 16. Once–
time; 17. really–degree; 18. nearby–place; 19. very–
degree; 20. totally–degree

Page 99
Lesson 8-1 Assessment
1. a; 2. c; 3. b; 4. e/b; 5. e; 6. here, there, everywhere;
7. clearly, here; 8. near; 9. annually; 10. Yesterday,
proudly; 11. loudly–manner; 12. quickly–manner;
13. every–time; 14. Sometimes–degree; 15. excitedly–
manner; 16. often–degree; 17. really–degree;
18. too–degree; 19. energetically–manner; 20. daily–
time/degree

Page 100
Lesson 8-2 Practice Level A
1. T; 2. T; 3. F; 4. T; 5. T; 6. Y; 7. Y; 8. N; 9. Y; 10. N;
11. with bananas; 12. before the milk; 13. to drench the
bananas; 14. in the bowl; 15. on my spoon; 16. in my
mouth; 17. without bananas; 18. in my cereal;
19. about a few months back; 20. on a regular basis

Page 101
Lesson 8-2 Practice Level B
1. T; 2. F; 3. F; 4. T; 5. T; 6. Y; 7. Y; 8. Y; 9. Y; 10. N;
11. Every single month; 12. to buy new clothes; 13. to
buy clothes for her sisters; 14. with her own money;
15. every week; 16. from her paychecks; 17. on Friday;
18. At the end of the month/to see how much she
earned; 19. to go shopping; 20. to buy clothes

Page 102
Lesson 8-2 Assessment
1. T; 2. T; 3. F; 4. T; 5. T; 6. Y; 7. Y; 8. Y; 9. N; 10. Y; 11. by
my father; 12. for the whole family; 13. in the back;
14. like an apple; 15. as bright as the sun; 16. by the
front door; 17. out the window; 18. as exciting as
Christmas; 19. in a long time; 20. for a ride

Answer Key

Pages 103–104

Lesson 8-3 Practice

1. N; 2. Y; 3. N; 4. N; 5. Y; 6. no; 7. nothing; 8. no one; 9. nothing; 10. barely; 11. no/any; 12. never/ever; 13. never/ever; 14. nothing/anything; 15. no/any; 16. barely/really; 17. never/ever; 18. nothing/anything; 19. never/ever; 20. nothing/anything

Pages 105–106

Lesson 8-3 Assessment

1. Y; 2. N; 3. Y; 4. Y; 5. Y; 6. rarely; 7. none; 8. never; 9. no; 10. nobody; 11. nobody/never–ever; 12. never/ever; 13. rarely/never–ever; 14. doesn't/no one–anyone; 15. isn't/no–any; 16. don't/nothing–anything; 17. don't/never–ever; 18. can't/no–any; 19. isn't/no–any OR a; 20. don't/ nothing–anything

Pages 107–108

Lesson 9-1 Practice Level A

1. Y; 2. N; 3. N; 4. Y; 5. Y; 6. a; 7. c; 8. b; 9. a; 10. b; 11. or; 12. and; 13. or; 14. but; 15. but; 16. so; 17. and; 18. and; 19. yet; 20. but

Pages 109–110

Lesson 9-1 Practice Level B

1. for; 2. so; 3. but; 4. g; 5. d; 6. b; 7. d, f; 8. c; 9. e; 10. a; 11. and; 12. nor; 13. so; 14. but; 15. for; 16. yet; 17. so; 18. and; 19. and; 20. so

Pages 111–112

Lesson 9-1 Assessment

1. but; 2. so; 3. and; 4. d, f; 5. e; 6. g; 7. a; 8. c; 9. b; 10. d; 11. but, yet; 12. and; 13. but; 14. so; 15. and; 16. nor; 17. and; 18. but; 19. and; 20. or

Page 113

Lesson 9-2 Practice Level A

1. N; 2. Y; 3. Y; 4. N; 5. Y; 6. either/whether; 7. as; 8. both; 9. or; 10. not only; 11. either; 12. Neither; 13. as; 14. but; 15. as; 16. whether; 17. but; 18. not only; 19. or; 20. or

Page 114

Lesson 9-2 Practice Level B

1. either/or; 2. neither/nor; 3. both/and; 4. not only/but also; 5. whether/or; 6. either/or; 7. whether/or; 8. neither/nor; 9. both/and; 10. not/but; 11. but; 12. or; 13. either; 14. either; 15. Both; 16. Not only; 17. whether; 18. or; 19. but; 20. not

Page 115

Lesson 9-2 Assessment

1. N; 2. N; 3. Y; 4. Y; 5. Y; 6. or; 7. neither; 8. both; 9. or; 10. not; 11. but also; 12. Either; 13. or; 14. Neither; 15. Not only; 16. but; 17. or; 18. Whether; 19. either; 20. both

Pages 116–117

Lesson 9-3 Practice

1. F; 2. T; 3. F; 4. F; 5. T; 6. d; 7. b; 8. a; 9. a; 10. a; 11. Goodness–negative or positive; 12. Oh no–negative; 13. Man–negative; 14. Argh–negative; 15. Aw–positive; 16. Hey–positive; 17. Oh yeah–positive; 18. Sweet–positive; 19. Yes–positive; 20. Man–negative or positive

Pages 118–119

Lesson 9-3 Assessment

1. T; 2. T; 3. F; 4. T; 5. F; 6. Ew; 7. Whew; 8. Yippee; 9. Eek; 10. No way; 11. ouch–negative; 12. Argh–negative; 13. Duh–negative; 14. Yes–negative; 15. Well–negative; 16. Ouch–negative; 17. Great–positive; 18. Hey–negative; 19. Ooh–negative; 20. Oops–negative